DISCRIMINATION IN AMERICA

BY DUCHESS HARRIS, JD, PHD

WITH KRISTIN MARCINIAK

CONTENT CONSULTANT

HEATH FOGG DAVIS, PHD
DIRECTOR, GENDER, SEXUALITY,
AND WOMEN'S STUDIES PROGRAM
TEMPLE UNIVERSITY

BEING
LGBTQ
IN AMERICA

Essential Library

An Imprint of Abdo Publishing | abdobooks.com

ABDOBOOKS.COM

Published by Abdo Publishing, a division of ABDO, PO Box 398166, Minneapolis, Minnesota 55439. Copyright © 2020 by Abdo Consulting Group, Inc. International copyrights reserved in all countries. No part of this book may be reproduced in any form without written permission from the publisher. Essential Library™ is a trademark and logo of Abdo Publishing.

Printed in the United States of America, North Mankato, Minnesota.
042019
092019

Cover Photos: John Wollwerth/Shutterstock Images, (cake); Nancy Beijersbergen/ Shutterstock Images, (couple)
Interior Photos: iStockphoto, 4–5, 6, 10, 17, 29, 49, 57, 69; People Images/ iStockphoto, 14–15; Matthew Staver/The Washington Post/Getty Images, 21; Ververidis Vasilis/Shutterstock Images, 23; John Hanna/AP Images, 27; BSIP/UIG/ Universal Images Group/Getty Images, 37; Monkey Business Images/Shutterstock Images, 40, 63; Hannah Peters/Getty Images News/Getty Images, 44; Jack Milton/ Portland Press Herald/Getty Images, 47; Rawpixel.com/Shutterstock Images, 51; Kathryn Scott Osler/The Denver Post/Getty Images, 53; Monkey Business Images/ iStockphoto, 61; Amanda Edwards/WireImage/Getty Images, 67; Media Photos/ iStockphoto, 73; Hafizussalam bin Sulaiman/Shutterstock Images, 77; Chris Allan/ Shutterstock Images, 81; Red Line Editorial, 83; Jacob Biba/The Washington Post/ Getty Images, 86; Alex Milan Tracy/Sipa USA/AP Images, 88–89; Frederick M. Brown/ Rich Fury/Human Rights Campaign (HRC)/Getty Images Entertainment/Getty Images, 90; Mike Coppola/Getty Images Entertainment/Getty Images, 93; Spencer Platt/Getty Images News/Getty Images, 96

Editor: Megan Ellis
Series Designer: Melissa Martin

LIBRARY OF CONGRESS CONTROL NUMBER: 2018966065

PUBLISHER'S CATALOGING-IN-PUBLICATION DATA

Names: Harris, Duchess, author | Marciniak, Kristin, author.
Title: LGBTQ discrimination in America / by Duchess Harris and Kristin Marciniak
Description: Minneapolis, Minnesota : Abdo Publishing, 2020 | Series: Being LGBTQ in America | Includes online resources and index.
Identifiers: ISBN 9781532119057 (lib. bdg.) | ISBN 9781532173233 (ebook)
Subjects: LCSH: LGBTQ people--Juvenile literature. | Anti-GLBT bias--Juvenile literature. | Sexual orientation discrimination--Juvenile literature. | Homophobic attitudes--Juvenile literature.
Classification: DDC 306.760--dc23

CONTENTS

1 A Hostile Atmosphere
4

2 Political Framework
14

3 Employment
26

4 Health Care
36

5 Education
46

6 Housing
56

7 The Criminal Justice System
66

8 Effects of Discrimination
76

9 Fighting against Discrimination
88

Essential Facts   100   Source Notes   106
Glossary   102   Index   110
Additional Resources   104   About the Authors   112

Many high school students attend dances such as prom, but not all high schools allow same-sex couples to attend together.

A HOSTILE ATMOSPHERE

A t McKinley High School in Buffalo, New York, only seniors are allowed to go to prom. Byshop Elliott, a junior at the school during the 2016–2017 school year, didn't mind that. But he did mind the rules about which couples were allowed to attend prom together. Between 2014 and 2016, the school principal enforced a policy that allowed only opposite-sex couples at school dances. Students purchasing couples' tickets had to provide the name of their date. Those with same-sex partners were denied tickets. Members of same-sex couples could buy individual tickets to the dance, but they were not allowed to dance together. If they tried, they were separated by the principal. Some were told they would be disciplined.

Elliott didn't think that was fair. Neither did same-sex couples who had attempted to attend school dances together. According to a complaint that the New York Civil Liberties Union filed on Elliott's behalf, students felt "humiliated and

excluded from some of the most prominent and popular school-wide social events of the year."[1]

Prom wasn't the only issue addressed in Elliott's federal lawsuit against Buffalo Public Schools. Since 2014, he had tried to establish a gay-straight alliance (GSA), sometimes called a gender-sexuality alliance, at his high school. GSAs are student-run clubs where lesbian, gay, bisexual, transgender, and queer (LGBTQ) students and allies can discuss issues regarding sexual orientation and gender identity. In most cases, GSAs are safe spaces where everyone is welcome to escape the pressures of high school life. But Elliott's attempts to form a GSA were either denied or ignored by the school's principal.

GSAs participate in community events such as Pride parades.

The principal's refusal was indicative of the broader school culture. "There is an atmosphere of hostility and bullying," said Destinee, a McKinley student.[2] Destinee, who identifies as genderfluid, said many LGBTQ students at the school felt they had to hide who they were to avoid prejudice and harassment. Elliott agreed. "Everyone should have a chance to feel included and excited about high school, including LGBTQ students," Elliott told CNN.[3]

LEGAL PRECEDENT FOR SAME-SEX DATES

As of 2019, many same-sex couples can attend school dances together without controversy. That's in part because of Aaron Fricke. In 1980, Fricke asked another gay student to prom. The student said yes, but their principal said no. He was concerned the teens would be targets of harassment and violence. The US District Court of Rhode Island ruled in Fricke's favor. Judge Raymond Pettine said prohibiting same-sex couples from attending a dance together violated their freedom of speech as outlined in the First Amendment of the Constitution. The school provided extra security, and the couple was allowed to dance the night away.

Elliott's lawsuit against Buffalo Public Schools was settled in Elliott's favor in September 2017. The school district oversaw the creation of the GSA. It provided antidiscrimination training for staff and students. It also posted notices about the district's existing antidiscrimination policies. This included language meant to protect LGBTQ students. Just days after the lawsuit was filed, the school district welcomed couples of all sexual orientations and gender identities to the senior prom.

DISCRIMINATION IN THE 2000s

Discrimination is the unjust treatment of a person or group of people because of an identifying characteristic, such as race, age, or gender. In the 1950s and 1960s, the civil rights movement sought political, financial, educational, and legal equality for African Americans and other people of color. That was followed in the 1960s and 1970s by the women's rights movement. It pushed for equal rights based on sex. Neither of these movements completely eradicated injustice, but they made a lasting impact on the rights of these groups of people.

In the 1990s and 2000s, civil rights activists turned their attention to the LGBTQ community. However, the LGBTQ community encompasses a wide variety of identities and experiences. This includes people who experience discrimination based on their gender identity and their sexuality. Some people experience discrimination because of their attraction to people of the same sex. Others who are transgender, or trans, have a gender identity that is different from the sex they were assigned at birth. They experience discrimination that cisgender, or cis, people do not. A cisgender person has a gender identity that is the same as the sex they were assigned at birth.

People in the LGBTQ community have fought for a long time to receive the same opportunities as heterosexual and cisgender people in the United States. For many, change has been slow. As of early 2019, there are no federal laws that explicitly protect the rights of LGBTQ people in the United States. Because of that, many acts of discrimination against people because of their sexuality or gender identity are technically legal.

PREJUDICE DOES NOT EQUAL DISCRIMINATION

Discrimination is an act a person chooses to take. It shouldn't be confused with prejudice, which is a preconceived, unfavorable opinion about a person or group. Prejudice is an attitude. While some prejudices exist from birth, many are influenced by the beliefs of family and friends or negative personal experiences. Everyone has prejudices to some extent. But having a prejudice doesn't mean one should discriminate. It is entirely possible to keep one's feelings and opinions private while treating others with fairness and dignity.

TYPES OF DISCRIMINATION

There are two different types of discrimination. Direct discrimination is when a person is treated negatively because of a specific physical or mental characteristic. Prohibiting same-sex couples from attending prom together and withholding approval of LGBTQ-specific clubs are examples of direct discrimination. Direct discrimination often stems from misinformation or negative stereotypes about a specific group of people. For example, some people believe that trans women are sexual predators. These people believe that for this reason,

LGBTQ people may experience harassment and bullying because of their sexuality or gender identity.

trans women should not be allowed to use women's restrooms in public. This belief is based on negative stereotypes about trans women and does not have any basis in fact.

Direct discrimination can take many forms. LGBTQ people can be denied jobs or promotions. Landlords can refuse to rent to them. Banks can reject loan applications. Businesses can even refuse customers. That's what happened to Jack Zawadski of Picayune, Mississippi. In 2016, Zawadski's partner of 52 years, Robert Husky, died after a lengthy illness. Prior to his passing, the couple's nephew arranged for Husky's funeral service and cremation. After Husky died, the funeral home refused to honor its commitment. According to a lawsuit filed against the funeral home, Zawadski was told he would have to find other arrangements for Husky's body. The funeral home did not "deal with their kind."[4]

The second type of discrimination is indirect discrimination. This occurs when a person is harmed because they were treated the same as everyone else. It may be less visible. However, it can be just as damaging as direct discrimination. For example, several states require that the gender marker on a person's driver's license match the gender marker on their birth certificate unless they can show a court order, an amended birth certificate, or proof of surgery. This causes problems for trans people who don't have the resources or desire for medical procedures and legal intervention. It also affects people born in the three states—Kansas,

MULTIPLE LABELS IN THE LGBTQ COMMUNITY

People in the LGBTQ community aren't defined by a single thing, such as the color of their skin or their nation of origin. Instead, this community encompasses related but separate areas: sexual orientation and gender identity. Because of that, some people within the community describe themselves with more than one label. For example, a transgender woman may also be attracted to both men and women. She's not just trans; she may also identify as bisexual. Conversely, a genderqueer or nonbinary person may be attracted only to members of one gender. They may self-identify as lesbian, gay, or straight.

THE INTERSECTION OF RACE, GENDER, AND SEXUALITY

According to a study cosponsored by Harvard University, nonwhite people in the LGBTQ community experience nearly double the discrimination of their white peers.[5] Researchers attribute this to what is known as intersectionality, or when different aspects of one's identity converge. The term *intersectionality* was created by scholar and activist Kimberlé Crenshaw. It originally referred to the struggles experienced by someone who is both black and a woman. Later, people began to use the term to refer to multiple, diverse categories that intersect, such as gender, ability, class, race, and sexuality.

Each person's identity shapes the way they are treated by the rest of the world. For example, a lesbian Latina may face discrimination not only from people outside the LGBTQ community because of her sexuality but also from people within the LGBTQ community who are biased against her ethnicity. Some LGBTQ rights activists are encouraging the community's members to be mindful of all LGBTQ experiences and not just those of cisgender white people.

Tennessee, and Ohio—that do not allow changes to original birth certificates. At best, these trans people may be subject to embarrassing and inappropriate questioning about their gender. At worst, they may be subjected to harassment and violence or denied access to public accommodations after being outed as trans.

THE IMPACT OF DISCRIMINATION

Discrimination negatively impacts one's health and well-being. According to a 2015 survey by the American Psychological Association (APA), only 31 percent of adults who have experienced discrimination say they are in excellent or very good health. Of adults who have not experienced discrimination, 45 percent say they are in excellent or very good health.[6] Even small acts of discrimination can cause feelings of stress and otherness. Over time, that can damage one's physical and mental health.

There are many physicians, mental health professionals, and support groups that can help people deal with the effects of discrimination. But advocates believe the best way to ensure the health and safety of the LGBTQ community is to stop discrimination before it starts. For some, that means educating people about the inaccuracies of harmful stereotypes. Others focus on altering the political framework that allows LGBTQ discrimination in the first place. They believe that changing laws and public representation in government is the way to stop LGBTQ discrimination in America.

DISCUSSION STARTERS

- How are same-sex couples treated in your school? Do you agree with how they are treated? Why or why not?

- Has someone you know experienced discrimination based on how they identify? If so, how did they respond?

- How do you identify? What types of discrimination have you experienced based on this, if any?

In some states, LGBTQ people can be fired from their jobs based on their gender identity or sexual orientation.

POLITICAL FRAMEWORK

n many places in the United States, it is legal to discriminate against someone because of their sexual orientation or gender identity. That's because there are no federal laws that explicitly prohibit people from doing so.

Some government organizations, such as the Equal Employment Opportunity Commission (EEOC), say laws that prohibit sex-based discrimination also apply to people who face discrimination because of their gender identity or sexual orientation. They believe discrimination based on one's own beliefs about how men and women should behave is sex discrimination. It relies on perceptions of femininity and masculinity, such as the ideas that women should appear feminine and men should only be attracted to women. Several federal courts have agreed with this interpretation. Court rulings do not change the wording of a law. But they can set a precedent for how to interpret a law in future cases.

Not everyone agrees with broad interpretations of antidiscrimination law. Some government entities, including the US Department of Justice and the US Department of Education under President Donald Trump's administration, believe laws should be interpreted exactly as written. This means that the term *sex* in any existing laws would only refer to the sex a person was assigned at birth. These agencies insist that laws against sex discrimination weren't written with the intent of protecting LGBTQ people. In order to protect the LGBTQ community, Congress would need to pass legislative amendments that explicitly say discrimination based on sexual orientation and gender identity is illegal.

THE GENERATIONAL DIVIDE

According to a 2017 survey cosponsored by Harvard University, approximately 90 percent of LGBTQ people think members of the LGBTQ community face discrimination in the United States. Those who are 50 or older think individual prejudice causes discrimination. Those who are 18–49 are more likely to think discriminatory laws and policies deserve as much blame as prejudiced beliefs.[1]

STATE ANTIDISCRIMINATION LAWS

Some states do explicitly protect LGBTQ populations. As of February 2019, 21 states have laws that ban discrimination in employment, housing, and public accommodations based on

Same-sex couples can foster and adopt children in some states but may be denied by private adoption agencies in other states.

sexual orientation and gender identity. Wisconsin has such laws about sexual orientation but not gender identity. Pennsylvania and Michigan do not have explicit legal protections for LGBTQ people, but each has a civil rights–related commission that interprets existing laws in a way that prohibits discrimination based on sexual orientation and gender identity. However, those interpretations are not a guarantee of protections for LGBTQ people.[2]

Twenty-six states provide no protection against LGBTQ discrimination. They are mostly in the South and the Upper Midwest. Some states even have laws that make it easier for people to discriminate against others based on their sexuality

RELIGIOUS DISCRIMINATION AND MASTERPIECE CAKESHOP

The Department of Justice is part of the executive branch of government. It cannot dictate court rulings. However, it can exert its influence by supporting defendants who are accused of discrimination. It did that in the 2017 Supreme Court case *Masterpiece Cakeshop v. Colorado Civil Rights Commission*.

In 2012, Charlie Craig and David Mullins tried to buy a wedding cake from Colorado baker Jack Phillips. Phillips said making a cake for a same-sex wedding was against his religious beliefs. The Colorado Civil Rights Commission said that Phillips violated the state's antidiscrimination law. The Colorado Supreme Court upheld that ruling. Phillips then brought his case to the US Supreme Court. In June 2018, the Supreme Court made a 7–2 ruling and overturned the previous decisions. The justices did not determine whether Phillips was breaking the law by refusing to make the cake. Instead, they said that Phillips had been mistreated during formal government hearings. One of the members of the Civil Rights Commission had referred to the use of religious beliefs to justify discrimination as "despicable."[4] The Supreme Court interpreted this as mistreatment, allowing Phillips to win his case.

and gender identity. In Alabama, Kansas, Michigan, Mississippi, North Dakota, Oklahoma, South Carolina, South Dakota, Texas, and Virginia, it is legal for child welfare agencies to refuse to provide services to families if it would go against the agencies' religious beliefs. That can make it very difficult for LGBTQ families to foster and adopt children in need. In Illinois and Tennessee, medical professionals can refuse service to LGBTQ patients. In Kansas, businesses can refuse to serve married same-sex couples. Some states, including Arkansas, Tennessee, and North Carolina, have statewide laws that prevent cities and counties from passing laws against LGBTQ discrimination.[3]

A MATTER OF POLITICS

Political ideologies shape the way people feel about certain issues. People who identify as liberal believe the government should support social and political change. Many liberals belong to the Democratic Party. Conservatives favor traditional values and attitudes. They advocate for less government interference. Many conservatives also believe it is the government's job to preserve the morality of the United States. Many conservatives belong to the Republican Party.

In general, liberals advocate for laws that protect all people. Conservatives are less likely to do so. This is reflected in state laws. States that consistently elect officials from the Democratic Party, such as California and Colorado, are the ones with laws against LGBTQ discrimination. States that consistently elect officials from the Republican Party, such as Arkansas and North Dakota, have historically resisted that type of legislation. For example, in February 2018, a subcommittee in the Virginia House of Delegates reviewed four bills prohibiting LGBTQ discrimination in employment and housing. The committee did not allow the House to debate the bills. Committee members said that bills that protected LGBTQ people would infringe on other people's right to religious freedom. That same month, a similar bill in Arizona did not make it past the committee.

RELIGIOUS EXEMPTIONS

The First Amendment of the Constitution guarantees that people in the United States can follow any religion. This provision was written to guarantee the separation of church and state. Churches can't tell the government what to do, and the government can't persecute people for their religious beliefs.

Twenty-one states have religious-exemption laws. These laws allow people, churches, nonprofit organizations, and sometimes corporations to violate laws that "burden their religious beliefs."[5] For example, a florist may decide that providing flowers for same-sex weddings is a violation of their religious beliefs. Denying service in a state without religious-exemption laws would be illegal. Doing so in a state with exemption laws would be legal.

Historically, organizations that accept federal funding are not allowed to discriminate against someone based on that person's religion or sexuality. These organizations include public schools and social service institutions. But in January 2019, the Department of Health and Human Services (HHS) under the Trump administration granted a waiver that allowed a federally funded foster care program in South Carolina to discriminate against volunteers and prospective foster families who did not identify as Christian. The organization, Miracle Hill, could turn away Jewish and LGBTQ foster families because those families did not follow the organization's religious beliefs. Opponents to the waiver believe such measures will harm children in need of support. It may also open the door for other federally funded organizations to discriminate against the LGBTQ community.

Jack Phillips, owner of Masterpiece Cakeshop, argued that making a cake for a same-sex wedding violated his religious beliefs.

LGBTQ RIGHTS IN THE TRUMP ERA

Political ideologies, or systems of beliefs, also influence the policies of presidential administrations. The administration of Barack Obama was a vocal proponent of LGBTQ rights during its tenure in the White House. In 2011, President Obama oversaw the military's repeal of Don't Ask, Don't Tell (DADT). Under DADT, gay and lesbian service members had to keep their sexual orientation a secret or risk being discharged. In June 2015, a display of rainbow lights shined on the exterior of the White House to celebrate the Supreme Court's ruling on *Obergefell v. Hodges*, which legalized same-sex marriage in the United States. In 2016, the Department of Defense, also known as the Pentagon, announced that currently enlisted trans service members could

MAJOR STEPS FORWARD IN POLITICAL REPRESENTATION

Out of the more than 400 LGBTQ candidates who ran for federal, state, and local political office in the 2018 federal and state midterm elections, a record 161 won.[6] Their road to government office wasn't easy. Many had to deal with prejudice and harassment along the way. For example, a Republican precinct committeeman in Kansas referred to Democratic congressional candidate Sharice Davids as a "radical socialist kick boxing lesbian Indian" and said she would be "sent back packing to the reservation."[7] Davids's supporters adopted what was meant to be a slur as a rallying cry to celebrate their candidate's diverse background. Her victory over Republican incumbent Kevin Yoder made her the first openly gay person to represent Kansas in the US Congress.

The Obama administration oversaw many different pro-LGBTQ bills and executive orders.

be open about their gender identity. Trans recruits could enlist at the beginning of 2018.

However, the Trump administration is more conservative than the Obama administration. Since Trump took office in 2017, his administration has attempted to undo many policies that positively impacted LGBTQ people. In its first year, the Trump administration said that LGBTQ people were not protected from discrimination in the workplace. It also voided the previous administration's guidance on protecting trans students. In August 2017, Trump directed the Pentagon to reverse the Obama-era policy that allowed trans people to serve openly in the military. In January 2019, the US Supreme Court allowed the reversal to go into effect while court cases challenging

THE IMPACT OF LGBTQ VOTERS

Approximately 4.5 percent of the US adult population is in the LGBTQ community. They represent 5 percent of eligible American voters. Although that number seems small, it accounts for 10 million votes.[9] That can make a big difference during close local, state, and federal races. LGBTQ voters tend to be liberal and support Democratic candidates. Lucas Acosta is the LGBTQ media director for the Democratic National Committee. Acosta says the Democratic Party is rooted in "commitment to inclusion and opportunity."[10]

However, not all LGBTQ people are liberals. The Log Cabin Republicans (LCR) is an organization for conservative LGBTQ people and their allies. In addition to supporting limited government and low taxes, LCR works within the Republican Party to educate their fellow conservatives about the need for inclusion of all people, no matter their sexual orientation or gender identity.

the ban were heard by lower courts.

Policies to protect people based on their gender identity continued to be removed in many other departments. In 2018, the Department of Education began rejecting cases from students who were denied access to public school restrooms that matched their gender identity. And according to a memo leaked from the Department of Health and Human Services (HHS) in October 2018, the Trump administration planned to change the legal definition of the word *gender*. The new definition would be "a biological, immutable condition determined by genitalia at birth."[8] This would mean that a person's gender would be based on their physical appearance at birth. However, this definition contradicts widely approved scientific and medical evidence about the nature of gender and identity. "This takes a position that what the medical community understands about their patients . . . is irrelevant because the government disagrees," says Catherine E. Lhamon.[11] Lhamon was the Obama-era leader of the Department of Education's Office for Civil Rights.

Although more people in the LGBTQ community were elected to public office in 2018 than ever before, trans people and their allies fear that redefining the legal meaning of gender will result in continued discrimination in health care, employment, education, and the judicial system. According to Sarah Warbelow, legal director of the Human Rights Campaign (HRC), "Transgender people are frightened. At every step where the [Trump] administration has had the choice, they've opted to turn their back on transgender people."[12]

DISCUSSION STARTERS

- Does your state have any protections for people based on sexuality? What about gender identity? If so, what are they? If not, why do you think that is the case?

- How has the federal government's approach to the LGBTQ community changed between the Obama and Trump administrations?

- What type of political ideology do you identify with? How does that influence your opinions about antidiscrimination laws?

3

In 2019, Kansas governor Laura Kelly, *seated*, signed an executive order that banned discrimination against LGBTQ state employees and contractors.

EMPLOYMENT

Workers in the United States are protected from discrimination by Title VII of the Civil Rights Act of 1964. Title VII states that employers cannot "discriminate against any individual with respect to his compensation, terms, conditions, or privileges of employment, because of such individual's race, color, religion, sex, or national origin."[1] That means workers can't be fired, paid less, or treated differently because of the color of their skin, which religion they follow, or where they're from.

Less clear is the meaning of the word *sex*. According to the EEOC, *sex* encompasses not only biological attributes that determine sex at birth, such as genitalia, but also sexual orientation and gender identity. The US Supreme Court and several federal courts agree. They have historically ruled in favor of people who experienced workplace discrimination because of their gender identity or sexuality. Other government agencies disagree. They argue members of the LGBTQ community are not protected by Title VII.

THE LGBTQ WAGE GAP

There has always been an employment gap between cis men and women. As of 2017, women were earning an average of 20 percent less than men who held the exact same job. Yet there is another, often overlooked, cause of wage disparities in the cisgender workforce: sexual orientation. According to a 2015 article in the *Atlantic*, cisgender heterosexual men are at the top of the earnings hierarchy in the United States. Gay men have the next highest salaries, followed by lesbians, then cis heterosexual women.[3]

In 2014, President Obama signed an executive order that protected federal employees and contractors from LGBTQ employment discrimination. Shortly after taking office in 2017, President Trump announced that policy would remain intact. It is one of the few Obama-era pro-LGBTQ policies that the Trump administration had not rolled back as of January 2019.

FORMS OF EMPLOYMENT DISCRIMINATION

According to a 2017 survey by workplace advocates Out and Equal, 25 percent of people in the LGBTQ community experienced employment discrimination in the past five years.[2] That means they were denied a job, refused a promotion or a raise, paid less, or fired. Even though 21 states and Washington, DC, have laws prohibiting such discrimination, it can happen anywhere.

LGBTQ employment discrimination also occurs when people are made to feel unsafe in the workplace. This can be caused by a variety of things, including physical, verbal, and written harassment. Jokes about a person's sexual orientation or gender identity are considered harassment, as are sexual advances. Trans employees may feel unsafe if they are not allowed to use the restroom of their choice. They may also feel threatened by intrusive questions.

Jameka Evans was a hospital security guard in Savannah, Georgia. She was subjected to several forms of discrimination

Some jobs, such as flight attendant and pilot, can have different uniforms based on the employee's gender.

during her year working at Georgia Regional Hospital. According to the lawsuit she filed in 2015, Evans was "denied equal pay or work, harassed, and physically assaulted or battered" because she was a lesbian. She was also discriminated against because she wore a "male uniform" and had a "male haircut."[4] Evans quit her job to escape the harassment.

Many LGBTQ employees try to lessen the risk of discrimination by staying "in the closet." This means they keep their sexual orientation or gender identity a secret. According to a 2018 report by the HRC, 46 percent of LGBTQ workers are not "out" at work.[5] Their top concerns were being stereotyped by coworkers, making others feel uncomfortable, and missing out on forming work relationships. Yet staying in the closet has its risks. Mental health professionals caution that hiding important aspects of one's identity can lead to low self-esteem, depression, and other mental health issues.

Not everyone has the luxury of deciding whether they come out at work or not. On Jessi Dye's first day of work at an Alabama nursing home in 2014, her manager called her into his office. He asked, "What are you?" Dye, a transgender woman, later said the question made her feel like she had been "punched in the stomach." Her manager had realized there was a difference between her appearance and the gender marker on her driver's license. "What am I supposed to do with you?" the manager asked. Then he fired her.[6]

PROGRESS IN EMPLOYMENT PROTECTIONS

Dye and Evans both took legal action against their former employers. Dye filed a complaint of discrimination with the EEOC. She and her manager ended up settling out of court. Evans didn't fare as well. The lawsuit she filed against her former employer was dismissed by the US District Court for the Southern District of Georgia. The judge ruled that Title VII does not protect people from discrimination based on sexual orientation. Evans appealed to the Court of Appeals for the Eleventh Circuit and the US Supreme Court. The court of appeals agreed with Evans's employer. The Supreme Court declined to hear the case.

A month after the Court of Appeals for the Eleventh Circuit found Evans's employer not guilty, another appeals court ruled in favor of a lesbian plaintiff suing her employer for discrimination.

"DELAYING THE INEVITABLE"

The US Supreme Court didn't provide a reason for its refusal to hear Evans's case. According to Greg Nevins of Lambda Legal, which represented Evans, the highest court in the nation is "delaying the inevitable." Since lower courts disagree on the legality of LGBTQ employment discrimination, it will eventually be up to the Supreme Court to settle the matter. Nevins is cautiously optimistic. He told *USA Today* the refusal to hear Evans's case was "not a 'no,' but a 'not yet.'"[7]

US FEDERAL COURT SYSTEM

US SUPREME COURT

1 COURT
9 JUSTICES

Jameka Evans appealed the ruling of the Court of Appeals for the Eleventh Circuit to the US Supreme Court. The Supreme Court declined to hear her case.

US COURT OF APPEALS

13 COURTS
12 REGIONAL
1 FEDERAL
179 JUDGES

Jameka Evans appealed the ruling of the district court to the Court of Appeals for the Eleventh Circuit. The court of appeals ruled against Evans.

US DISTRICT COURTS

94 DISTRICTS IN 12 CIRCUITS
678 JUDGES

Jameka Evans filed a lawsuit against Georgia Regional Hospital in *Evans v. Georgia Regional Hospital*.
The case went to the US District Court for the Southern District of Georgia. The court ruled against Evans.

The US Supreme Court typically hears cases after they go through the lower courts first.

Kimberly Hively was an adjunct professor at Ivy Tech Community College in Indiana for 14 years. Hired as a part-time employee, she applied for full-time positions six times during her time at the college. She was denied every time. Eventually, the school refused to renew her contract. Hively was certain she was being discriminated against because of her sexual orientation. As in Evans's case, a lower court ruled that sexual orientation is not protected by Title VII. The US Court of Appeals for the Seventh Circuit disagreed in April 2017. At the time, it was the highest federal court to rule that employment discrimination based on sexual orientation is a violation of federal law.

Less than a year later, a second federal appeals court made a similar ruling. Donald Zarda was fired from his job as a skydiving instructor in 2010 after joking about his

LOCATION, LOCATION, LOCATION

Evans and Hively were both lesbians who sued for workplace-based discrimination because of their sexual orientation. So why did their appeals to district courts have different outcomes? It could be due to their location. Hively's appeal went to the Court of Appeals for the Seventh Circuit, which is in Chicago, Illinois. Illinois is a fairly liberal state and offers legal protections for LGBTQ employees. Evans's appeal went to the Court of Appeals for the Eleventh Circuit, which is in Atlanta, Georgia. Georgia is a conservative state. It generally does not recognize LGBTQ people as being protected from employment discrimination.

sexual orientation with a client. The client complained to her boyfriend, who reported it to Zarda's boss, who fired him. In February 2018, the US Court of Appeals for the Second Circuit reversed the initial ruling of a lower court to declare discrimination on the basis of sexual orientation illegal. The victory was bittersweet. Zarda had died four years earlier during a BASE jumping accident. BASE jumping is an extreme sport that involves a person jumping from a high point using a parachute. His former partner and his sister pursued the case on his behalf.

DIFFERENT INTERPRETATIONS

The 2017 and 2018 appeals court rulings indicate that some judges are taking a more expansive view of the protections granted by Title VII. LGBTQ civil rights advocates hope this sets a legal precedent for future cases of LGBTQ discrimination.

Despite these landmark cases, there are still courts and government entities that don't believe in a broad interpretation of Title VII. Because of this disparity in rulings by federal courts, in April 2019, the US Supreme Court agreed to hear arguments for three cases pertaining to LGBTQ employment discrimination and Title VII. One of these cases is *Zarda v. Altitude Express, Inc.* The Supreme Court's decision on these cases would determine whether *sex* in Title VII applies to gender identity and/or sexual orientation—and therefore, whether Title VII protects employees in the LGBTQ community.

DISCUSSION STARTERS

- How do you define the word *sex*? How is sex different from gender?

- Federal courts don't agree on employment protections for LGBTQ people. Why is that? What could change that?

Trans patients can seek gender-affirming surgeries from care providers, but not all doctors are willing to treat trans patients.

HEALTH CARE

O ne of the most important aspects of achieving and maintaining good health is finding an affordable health-care provider who understands a patient's needs. That can be difficult for members of the LGBTQ community. According to a 2017 study by Harvard University, 16 percent of LGBTQ people have experienced discrimination by a health-care provider because of their gender identity or sexual orientation.[1] For many LGBTQ people, the risk of discrimination is enough to prevent them from seeking medical care.

TYPES OF HEALTH-CARE DISCRIMINATION

Health-care discrimination ranges in severity and intent. In some cases, providers don't know how to relate to or treat patients who are not cisgender and heterosexual. For example, a provider may not know how to prescribe hormone replacement therapy (HRT) for trans patients wishing to medically transition. They may not know how to correctly refer

to a trans patient's gender and accidentally misgender them. That can make patients uncomfortable and unwilling to share information about their health.

DISPARITIES IN TRANS HEALTH CARE

The 2015 US Transgender Survey indicates that trans people face even greater health-care disparities than cisgender people in the LGBTQ community. One-third of the survey's respondents reported having at least one negative experience, such as verbal harassment or refusal of treatment, with a health-care provider in the past year. Approximately 23 percent of respondents avoided going to the doctor when they were ill out of fear of mistreatment. Approximately 33 percent didn't seek medical care because of the cost.[2]

Some trans and nonbinary people also avoid medical care because of providers' ignorance about what it means to be transgender. "They do not understand my body," queer writer and performer Sinclair Sexsmith writes in *The Remedy: Queer and Trans Voices on Health and Health Care*. "So why would I trust them to help me with my health and wellness?"[3]

Other providers may purposefully discriminate against LGBTQ patients. Some might refuse to prescribe specific treatments. Others may not take LGBTQ patients at all. In 2018, Hilde Hall, a trans woman from Arizona, was prescribed HRT by her doctor. She was excited about her transition. Her excitement turned into humiliation when she went to pick up her medication. The pharmacist at her local drugstore refused to fill one of the prescriptions. He kept loudly asking why she needed them. "I nearly started crying in the middle of the store," Hall wrote in a statement to the American Civil Liberties Union (ACLU). "I felt like the pharmacist was trying to out me as transgender in front of strangers."[4] Blatant acts of discrimination like this are often based on the provider's own negative feelings about people in the LGBTQ community. These feelings are usually rooted in religious beliefs.

LGBTQ PATIENTS IN MEDICAL EDUCATION

According to a 2011 review of LGBTQ content in medical education, medical students receive an average of five hours of LGBTQ-related training throughout their entire four years of medical school.[5] Many LGBTQ advocates argue that isn't nearly enough. That's why some medical schools are developing LGBTQ-specific programs. The first to do so was the University of Louisville School of Medicine in 2014. Since then, several other schools, including Harvard University and the University of Minnesota, have developed LGBTQ curricula for their students. These classes may be electives or core coursework during medical school.

HOW DISCRIMINATION AFFECTS HEALTH

Positive health outcomes, such as lower risks of disease and longer lives, are more likely when patients have open and trusting relationships with their health-care providers. But many patients become uncomfortable or embarrassed when discussing sex and sexuality. For LGBTQ patients, this discomfort is often related to the fear of being judged or mistreated because of their sexual orientation or

Affirming health-care providers can lead to improved health outcomes for LGBTQ patients.

gender identity. Because of that, they may not be honest about their identity or sexuality. That can impact a doctor's ability to properly diagnose ailments and provide preventative treatments. Alex, a 17-year-old trans woman, stopped discussing her gender identity and sexuality with health-care providers. Because of that, she was not offered certain screenings for sexually transmitted infections and preventative medications that applied to her sexual health. Though Alex was at high risk for contracting the human immunodeficiency virus (HIV), medical providers had never informed her about pre-exposure prophylaxis (PrEP), a daily pill that reduces the risk of contracting HIV.

Alex found this gap in her health care troubling. However, she had stopped disclosing her gender identity and sexuality with health-care providers because Alex found it exhausting. Occasionally, providers were rude. Because of this discomfort, Alex lacked information that could keep her healthy.

Health outcomes are even worse when one avoids the doctor's office altogether. According to the Harvard study, 18 percent of people who identify as LGBTQ haven't sought medical care for an ailment because they feared discrimination.[6] Many members of the LGBTQ community also avoid visiting health-care providers for preventative care. This puts the LGBTQ population at higher risk of negative health outcomes, such as obesity, heart disease, diabetes, and certain forms of cancer.

ADDITIONAL BARRIERS

A person's location can also affect their ability

"WHAT DID WE JUST BRING THIS KID INTO?"

In 2015, Krista and Jami Contreras of Michigan brought their six-day-old daughter, Bay, to the doctor for her first checkup. Another doctor told them the pediatrician had "prayed on it" and decided she couldn't care for Bay because her mothers were lesbians.[7] The Contrerases are featured in a commercial for the Beyond I Do campaign, a national campaign sponsored by the Ad Council and the Gill Foundation. In it, Jami remembers the terror of that moment. "I wanted to cry just thinking, 'What did we just do? Like, what did we just bring this kid into?'"[8]

to access LGBTQ-friendly health care. Urban areas traditionally have more physicians and more health-care options than rural communities. In a 2017 survey by the Center for American Progress (CAP), 18 percent of LGBTQ respondents said it would be "very difficult" or "not possible" to find alternative health care if they were denied treatment at a hospital. For rural respondents, that number is 41 percent. This is partly because of anti-LGBTQ attitudes in some rural areas. It is also because of the lack of rural health-care providers in general. If the only physician in the area refuses to treat LGBTQ patients or won't provide certain services, the next closest option might be over 100 miles (160 km) away.[9]

Health insurance can also be a barrier to obtaining health care for people in the LGBTQ community. Health insurance is expensive. In 2015, an estimated 11 percent of nonheterosexual people were uninsured. Twenty-five percent of trans people were uninsured.[10] Some people in the LGBTQ community may not have access to policies that cover unmarried or domestic partners. Insurance companies may also deny coverage for specific treatments, such as HRT and gender-confirmation surgeries.

Some insurance companies may also deny coverage because of the medication a person is taking. In 2015, Dr. Philip J. Cheng cut himself while performing surgery on a patient living with HIV. To make sure he didn't contract HIV, Cheng took a one-month course of a PrEP medication called Truvada. After finishing the one-month course, Cheng continued taking Truvada to lessen the risk of contracting HIV during casual sexual encounters. But when Cheng applied for lifetime disability insurance, which would help cover his expenses if he became too ill to work, the insurance company only offered him a five-year policy because he was taking Truvada. "I was really shocked," Cheng told the *New York Times*. "PrEP is the responsible thing to do. It's the closest thing we have to an HIV vaccine."[11] Cheng stopped taking Truvada in order to get insurance from another company.

HIV STIGMA

Since its discovery in the early 1980s, HIV has largely been associated with gay men. Although methods of prevention, detection, and treatment have advanced greatly over the years, the stigma still remains. This is true even in the medical community. For example, in 2015 the US Food and Drug Administration relaxed its 20-year ban on blood and plasma donations from gay men. Now men who have not had sex with another man within a year can donate. While acknowledging this is "a step in the right direction," HRC spokesman David Stacy says any restriction at all stigmatizes gay and bisexual men. According to Stacy, prohibiting sexually active gay men from donating blood "cannot be justified in light of current scientific research and updated blood screen technology."[12]

WHERE WE ARE

Most major health-care organizations in the United States, including the American Medical Association and the American Academy of Pediatrics, have publicly taken a stance

Some trans people protest health-care discrimination.

against discrimination based on gender identity and sexual orientation. But as of January 2019, no federal laws prohibit health-care discrimination for LGBTQ patients. Only 14 states and Washington, DC, have any laws related to health-care discrimination for LGBTQ patients. All have to do with insurance coverage. No states have specific laws related to denial of service by health-care providers.

At the federal level, the Trump administration is focusing on protecting health-care professionals, not their LGBTQ patients.

According to an April 2018 article in the *New York Times*, administration officials are attempting to remove LGBTQ protections from the Affordable Care Act (ACA), also known as Obamacare. They argue that the Obama administration misinterpreted the meaning of the word *sex* in the ACA's antidiscrimination policies. Under the Obama administration's interpretation, doctors, hospitals, and health insurance companies could be penalized for discriminating against members of the LGBTQ community. If the Trump administration succeeds, health-care discrimination based on gender identity and sexual orientation would be legal in states that do not have laws that prohibit such acts.

In 2018, the Trump administration further protected health-care providers with the creation of the Conscience and Religious Freedom division of the HHS. It defends health-care providers who refuse to provide services that violate their religious or moral beliefs about birth control, abortion, and assisted suicide. LGBTQ advocates fear this office will also take the side of doctors who don't want to treat LGBTQ patients.

DISCUSSION STARTERS

- Do doctors' religious beliefs outweigh their duty to help patients? Why or why not?
- Were you worried about discrimination the last time you went to the doctor? Why or why not?

GSAs can help other students understand people in the LGBTQ community. They can also provide a safe space for students.

EDUCATION

School is supposed to be a safe place for all students to learn. That wasn't the case for LGBTQ students at North Bend High School (NBHS) in North Bend, Oregon. According to students Liv Funk and Hailey Smith, LGBTQ students at NBHS regularly endured verbal harassment and physical assault on and off school property. Instead of protecting LGBTQ students, some teachers and staff members joined in on the bullying. One teacher told Smith that marrying a person of the same sex was the equivalent of "marrying a dog."[1] Another made an LGBTQ student read aloud from the Bible as punishment.

Most LGBTQ students at NBHS were afraid to speak out against the school's culture of hate. But Funk and Smith had had enough. They took their concerns to a student-run legal clinic at Willamette University College of Law. Students there reported the discrimination to the Oregon Department of Education (ODE). After an investigation in early 2018, the ODE verified that "discrimination on the basis of sex and sexual orientation may have occurred" at NBHS.[2]

THE STUDENT NONDISCRIMINATION ACT

The Student Nondiscrimination Act was first introduced in Congress in 2015. Supported almost entirely by Democrats, the proposed law would prohibit discrimination and harassment of LGBTQ students, or students perceived as being in the LGBTQ community, at schools that receive public money. Institutions found in violation of the law would lose their public funding. The bill ultimately never made it out of subcommittees. It was reintroduced in the House of Representatives and the Senate in March 2018, where it was once again sent to committee for review.

This type of discrimination is illegal in Oregon. Oregon is one of 13 states, as well as Washington, DC, that prohibits bullying and discrimination based on sexual orientation and gender identity. However, the penalties for breaking the law were fairly light. The school district issued a written apology to Smith and Funk. It also donated $1,000 to a local LGBTQ support group and agreed to develop a "diversity and inclusion committee" to educate students and staff.[3] At NBHS, a resource officer was fired, and the principal was transferred to a different school.

ALIENATION AND ISOLATION

Anti-LGBTQ attitudes and actions in schools aren't all that unusual. According to the 2017 National School Climate Survey by GLSEN, an LGBTQ student-advocacy group, 87 percent

Gender expression is the physical expression of someone's gender identity. This may include wearing makeup, cutting their hair, or receiving gender-affirming surgery.

of LGBTQ students have experienced verbal harassment or physical assault while at school. Approximately 62 percent have been subjected to discriminatory practices. These range from being disciplined for wearing clothing that is "not appropriate" for one's birth gender to being barred from writing about LGBTQ topics for school assignments. Some students felt they had been punished "for being LGBTQ."[4]

Trans students fared even worse at school. Approximately 42 percent weren't allowed to use their preferred names

FREE SPEECH PROTECTIONS AT SCHOOL

The First Amendment of the US Constitution guarantees the right to free speech. This includes speech at public schools. LGBTQ students can talk about their sexual orientation or gender identity even if others don't like it. They can also distribute leaflets, hang posters, write newspaper articles, and wear clothing that expresses positive LGBTQ statements.

Free speech protections also apply to people who voice their opposition to LGBTQ civil rights, but they do not cover acts of harassment and discrimination. According to the ACLU, the difference is that "students do not have a right to express themselves if such expression substantially interferes with the rights of a classmate."[7] Harassment, assault, and discrimination violate a person's right to an equal education. Making a rational argument defending one's personal views does not.

and pronouns, and 47 percent had to use school restrooms that matched the sex they were assigned at birth.[5] In 2017, trans boy Drew Adams sued his Florida school district after Adams was told he could not use the men's restroom because it made another student uncomfortable. Adams had to use a gender-neutral bathroom, of which there were few on campus. "I feel alienated. I'm isolated. I'm separated from the rest of my classmates," Adams wrote in a 2017 blog post for Lambda Legal, an LGBTQ civil rights organization.[6] In the summer of 2018, a federal court ruled in Adams's favor. It was just in time for his senior year of high school.

EFFECTS OF EDUCATIONAL DISCRIMINATION

Discrimination can negatively impact a student's desire and ability to learn. According to the 2017 National School Climate Survey, LGBTQ students who experience harassment, violence, or discrimination at school have a lower grade point average than those who have not faced bullying or discrimination.

Students who are bullied because of their sexuality or gender identity may have a harder time later in life.

They miss more days of school. They're also more likely to drop out of school or forgo further education after high school.[8]

Educational discrimination can also damage a person's social and emotional well-being. In 2014, Doris Thompson received a letter from Timberlake Christian School (TCS) about her eight-year-old granddaughter, Sunnie Kahle. It suggested that Thompson should not enroll Kahle for the following school year. The letter stated that Kahle did not dress and act feminine enough. Thompson removed Kahle from the school immediately, but this upset Kahle. She liked her old school. Her friends there were all supportive of the way she expressed her gender. But the adults had a problem with her appearance and behavior. "[The administrators] pretty much ruined a little girl's life," Thompson

BLURRING OF CHURCH AND STATE

Even private religious schools receive some money from the government. For example, TCS gets taxpayer money through voucher programs. The government gives the amount of money it would have spent on a student's public school education to a private school of a family's choice. According to a 2017 investigation by *Huffpost,* more than 7,100 schools—many of which are religious—participate in school voucher programs or allow people to take tax credits for donations to schools' scholarship programs. Approximately 14 percent of those schools that also identify as religious enforce policies that actively discriminate against LGBTQ students.[9] LGBTQ civil rights advocates argue that this is a violation of federal law, but as of January 2019, no lawsuits against these voucher programs have been filed.

Religious private schools are allowed to refuse to admit students based on their gender expression, gender identity, or sexual orientation.

said in 2017.[10] According to her grandmother, Kahle has been depressed and angry ever since switching to her new school, where she is bullied and teased for her gender expression.

Thompson and Kahle live in Virginia, which does not have laws that protect LGBTQ students from bullying and discrimination. Even if it did, TCS would have been exempt. It is a private religious school. That means it can dictate who can attend its school and who can't. Public schools are not allowed to do that. They must follow the regulations set forth in Title IX, a federal law that bans sex discrimination in schools.

The problem is that much like in Title VII, not all states believe that the word *sex* includes a person's gender identity and sexual orientation.

Antibullying laws and nondiscrimination laws ensure the safety of LGBTQ students in school. As of March 2019, 24 states had no antibullying laws for gender identity or sexual orientation. Thirty-three states had no nondiscrimination laws protecting LGBTQ students. Some states interpret existing laws about sex discrimination to include sexual orientation and gender identity. But in other states, such as Missouri and South Dakota, it is illegal to create antibullying and antidiscriminatory policies at all.

Seven southern states, ranging from Arizona to South Carolina, have "Don't Say Gay" or "No Promo Homo" regulations for public schools. Some states prohibit teachers from presenting LGBTQ issues, including information about

HEALTH RISKS OF "NO PROMO HOMO" LAWS

"No Promo Homo" laws also have lasting effects on physical health. For example, six of the seven states with these laws have some of the highest rates of HIV diagnoses in the United States. Though many people associate HIV with gay men, anyone can contract it, regardless of gender identity or sexual orientation. Education about how it is transmitted is the key to protecting oneself. When states prohibit teachers from discussing sexual health and disease prevention, the risk of acquiring HIV is much higher.

sexual health, in a positive manner. Some specifically require that teachers only say negative things about LGBTQ people. And there are some states that forbid discussion of LGBTQ issues at all. For example, North Carolina law specifies that all reproductive health and safety classes must teach that "a mutually faithful monogamous *heterosexual* relationship in the context of marriage is the best lifelong means of avoiding sexually transmitted diseases, including HIV/AIDs."[11]

Policies like these are enormously harmful. Educators who spread misinformation about the LGBTQ community (or ignore it altogether) perpetuate the stigma and stereotypes associated with being an LGBTQ person. This creates an atmosphere where prejudice and discrimination against the LGBTQ community are normal. It can lead to feelings of isolation, depression, and despair for LGBTQ students and adults.

DISCUSSION STARTERS

- Should the First Amendment apply to private religious schools? Why or why not?

- Have you seen someone being bullied at school for their gender identity or sexual orientation? What happened? What was done to stop it?

- Why is it important to have both nondiscrimination and antibullying laws? Why is it important to have laws that refer to both gender identity and sexual orientation?

6

Same-sex couples who want to live together may have a difficult time finding houses to buy or rent due to housing discrimination.

HOUSING

Housing is one of humankind's basic needs. But for members of the LGBTQ community, safe and affordable housing can be difficult to secure if landlords, sellers, or lenders are aware of the person's sexual orientation or gender identity. That was the case for Queen, a trans woman from North Carolina. She never had problems with her landlord until he entered her apartment to fix a leak. While there, he noticed Queen's rainbow flag and some equality stickers. Two weeks later, the landlord told Queen that her building was being sold and she needed to move out. Queen moved in with family until she could find another apartment.

Later, Queen found out the landlord didn't sell the building at all. He just didn't want her living there because she was trans. "Having so many doors closed makes you want to give up on yourself," Queen said to equality website Beyond I Do.[1]

DISCRIMINATION AGAINST LGBTQ PEOPLE EXPERIENCING HOMELESSNESS

Discrimination in housing policies, income disparities, and unsupportive families have forced many LGBTQ people into homelessness. Most major urban areas have support systems for people experiencing homelessness. These include shelters, soup kitchens, and outreach programs. The US Department of Housing and Urban Development's Equal Access Rule (EAR) makes it illegal for assistance programs receiving government money to discriminate against LGBTQ people.

While helpful, the law has one major flaw: EAR does not specify that trans people have the right to stay in housing that aligns with their gender identity. Assigning people to housing that matches their birth sex instead of their gender identity puts trans people at greater risk of harassment and violence. Skylar came out as trans while living in a Wisconsin homeless shelter in 2017. Although the staff tried to be accommodating, she wasn't allowed to use the women's facilities. "Some people called me names and even outright got in my face and with hostile comments," she said.[2] Private shelters, particularly those associated with conservative churches, are even less likely to accommodate the needs of LGBTQ people. They may enforce the separation of same-sex couples or deny services altogether.

THE REALITY OF HOUSING DISCRIMINATION

Housing discrimination is when one person refuses to rent or sell to or buy property from another person based on appearance or another identifying characteristic. This includes denying housing loans based on anything other than financial status, as well as changing the price or rent of a house depending on who the buyer is.

The Fair Housing Act protects most people in the United States. It prohibits housing discrimination based on a person's race, color, national origin, religion, sex, and disability. It also forbids discrimination based on family status, such as whether a couple is married or has children. As with many other federal civil rights laws, the Fair Housing Act does not mention gender identity or sexual orientation. However, there are instances where discriminating against someone because of their identity or orientation is illegal. For example, while it is legal to evict a gay man from his apartment because he is gay, it is illegal to evict a gay man from his apartment because the landlord thinks he will expose other residents to HIV because of his sexuality. The difference is that in the second example, the eviction is based on the perception of a disability, which is what federal law considers HIV to be.

Fear of housing discrimination among LGBTQ people is widespread. A 2015 survey conducted by real estate professionals indicated that 73 percent of LGBTQ people were "strongly" concerned about discrimination by real estate agents, landlords, property sellers, and neighbors.[3]

Those fears are not unfounded. In 2017, the Urban Institute, a think tank that researches economic and social policy, conducted 1,200 tests of housing discrimination. Each test consisted of a pair of people. One person posed as half of a same-sex couple. The other person posed as half of a

"NO LGBT PEOPLE"

In 2016, Buddy Fisher used Airbnb to rent an Austin home for a short-term stay. When the site asked Fisher why he was visiting Austin, he mentioned he was going to the August Pride Parade. An hour later, the owner of the home canceled the reservation and messaged Fisher: "No LGBT people please. I do not support people who are against humanity. Sorry."[6]

Airbnb's nondiscrimination policy mentions a commitment to "inclusion and respect" that "enables every member of our community to feel welcome on the Airbnb platform no matter who they are, where they come from, how they worship, or whom they love."[7] The site ultimately removed the host's listing and banned him from using Airbnb. Even so, it was a low point for Fisher. "We take so many steps forward, but then we get knocked back with things like this," he told the *Houston Press*.[8]

heterosexual couple. Each pair separately visited the same housing agent. Researchers found that gay men were offered fewer appointments, shown fewer available units, and quoted higher rates than straight men. Lesbians fared better, but they were still offered fewer units than straight women.[4]

Another 200 tests had pairs pose as trans and cis people. Agents were less likely to tell trans applicants who disclosed their trans status about available units. Trans applicants who did not mention their gender identity were still shown fewer units than cis applicants.[5]

HEADWAYS FOR CHANGE

Federal law does not specifically protect LGBTQ people from housing discrimination. However, several federal courts have

LGBTQ people may face discrimination when buying houses. Agents may not show them available houses in order to keep them out of certain neighborhoods.

REALTORS DROP ANTI-LGBTQ CONGRESSMAN

In May 2018, California congressman Dana Rohrabacher said homeowners shouldn't have to do business with LGBTQ people if they "don't agree with their lifestyle." He further explained, "We've drawn a line on racism, but I don't think we should extend that line."[9] Rohrabacher's comments came after a meeting with the National Association of Realtors (NAR) where he was urged to consider federal housing protections for LGBTQ people. NAR subsequently dropped its endorsement of Rohrabacher. Months later, he lost his 2018 campaign for reelection.

recently ruled that the Fair Housing Act does apply to LGBTQ populations. As with Title VII, several judges have determined that the word *sex* in the Fair Housing Act also encompasses a person's sexual orientation.

The first such case to deal with gender identity was in 2017. A few years before, Rachel and Tonya Smith tried to rent a townhouse for their family in Boulder, Colorado. They toured the home and met the neighbors in the adjoining house. Everything went well. However, the landlord refused to rent to them. She said the neighbors were concerned about the noise the children might cause. The landlord also said she and her husband "kept a low profile" in town and didn't want to do anything to change that.

The Smiths were pretty sure the landlord was referring to Rachel, who is trans. "[The landlord] said because it was a small

Landlords may avoid renting properties to certain groups or classes of people. This is a form of housing discrimination.

town and everybody gossips. Our unique relationship . . . would be the talk of the town," Tonya said in an interview with the *Washington Post*.[10]

The Smiths were stunned. "I was really taken aback," Rachel said. "You can't do that. You can't say that to people. That's not okay."[11] US district judge Raymond P. Moore agreed. He ruled in favor of the Smiths in 2017.

The Court of Appeals for the Seventh Circuit made a similar ruling in 2018 for Martha Wetzel. Wetzel moved into a suburban Chicago, Illinois, senior living center in 2013. While there, she endured constant harassment and physical abuse from other tenants because of her sexual orientation. When she complained, the facility banned her from some of the center's common areas. Her harassers didn't face any consequences.

Wetzel's case against the senior living center was dismissed by a district court in 2017. Wetzel and Lambda Legal appealed that decision. The judges at the Court of Appeals for the Seventh Circuit ruled in Wetzel's favor. It was an important decision. It indicated that landlords are legally bound to protect their LGBTQ tenants from discrimination by other tenants.

WHERE WE ARE

As of February 2019, 21 states and Washington, DC, have laws that explicitly prohibit housing discrimination based on gender identity and sexual orientation. Housing discrimination still occurs in these places, but victims are able to get justice through the legal system. That isn't true for the 48 percent of LGBTQ people who live in the 26 states that have no LGBTQ housing protections.[12]

Some members of Congress are trying to make sure all LGBTQ people are protected from housing

SENATOR DRAWS ON EXPERIENCE AS FAIR-HOUSING ATTORNEY

The Equal and Fair Housing Act of 2017 was spearheaded by Democratic senator Tim Kaine of Virginia. Before becoming the governor of Virginia, Kaine was a fair-housing lawyer. He specialized in representing people who were denied housing based on race, disability, or family status. He now uses his political position to advocate for fair housing for veterans, low-income families, and the LGBTQ community.

discrimination. In March 2017, the Fair and Equal Housing Act of 2017 was introduced in the House of Representatives. A bill of the same title was introduced to the Senate that June. The bill would expand the Fair Housing Act "to add sexual orientation and gender identity as classes protected against discrimination in the sale, rental, or financing of housing."[13] Both bills were sent to subcommittees for further review. As of February 2019, the fates of those bills have not been decided.

DISCUSSION STARTERS

- Do you agree with the court's ruling that tenants be protected from discriminatory actions by landlords?

- What are some similarities between the experiences of young people in the LGBTQ community and the experience of older people, such as Wetzel? What are some differences?

- What are the consequences of not being able to find safe and affordable housing?

CeCe McDonald, *left*, experienced transphobia while in prison. A documentary about her incarceration was produced by Laverne Cox, *right*.

THE CRIMINAL
JUSTICE SYSTEM

The United States' criminal justice system was built on the idea that every person should be treated equally. In reality, that isn't always the case. Racial minorities, people living in poverty, and LGBTQ people often face bias and unfair treatment by police officers, the courts, and the prison system simply because of who they are.

This has led to a disproportionate number of LGBTQ criminal convictions and incarcerations. A 2011–2012 National Inmate Survey reported that nearly 8 percent of state and federal prison inmates self-identified as nonheterosexual. The same survey reported that 3.8 percent of people in the United States identified as LGBTQ.[1] This disparity comes from two sources: unfair policing practices and discrimination in legal proceedings.

GENDER SEGREGATION AND CECE MCDONALD

In 2011, trans woman CeCe McDonald and two of her friends were attacked outside a bar in Minneapolis, Minnesota. A man and two women hurled slurs and racial insults at McDonald and her friends. They also threw a glass, which shattered against McDonald's face. McDonald, a fashion student, pulled a pair of sewing shears out of her purse. She used them to defend herself when the man charged at her. He later died from his injuries.

The judge in McDonald's trial ignored all evidence of the attacker's bad intentions and character. The judge convicted McDonald of murder. McDonald was sent to a men's prison because of the sex marker on her birth certificate.

While in prison, McDonald wrote about the brutal treatment she endured. Her words inspired activists around the world. They started the #FreeCeCe movement to shed light on how the criminal justice system treats trans people. Upon her release in 2014, McDonald began speaking around the country about getting rid of prisons and addressing societal issues that lead to crime, such as poverty, addiction, homelessness, and lack of health care for mental health issues. The 2016 documentary *Free CeCe!* was produced by actress and trans activist Laverne Cox.

POLICE PROCEDURES AND COURT RULINGS

LGBTQ people are not more likely to engage in criminal activity than anyone else. Yet they are more likely to be arrested or charged with crimes. Experts believe this is due to the enforcement of outdated anti-LGBTQ laws and bias of officers. For example, many states have indecency laws that prohibit acts of nudity or public sexual activity. A gay couple violating those laws is more likely to be charged with a crime than a heterosexual couple would be because of the way prejudice and bias play into those types of decisions.

Law enforcement officials have also been known to target areas where LGBTQ people gather, such as LGBTQ-friendly bars or community centers. In these cases, police officers are not responding to complaints of criminal activity. They are instead actively seeking out infractions for which people could be arrested, such as city curfew violations or minor instances of

Judges and juries may be prejudiced against LGBTQ people. This can affect the outcomes of cases involving LGBTQ discrimination.

drug possession. LGBTQ people do not have to break laws to be ticketed. A 2011 New York City focus group of LGBTQ teens reported they were fined for resting their feet on subway seats, sitting in playgrounds after dark, and dressing "offensive[ly]."[2]

Anti-LGBTQ discrimination is also present within the courtroom. Prejudices from the judge, jury, or attorneys can impact the outcome of a case. That is what happened to Jessica Lynn, a trans woman. A court granted Lynn custody of her three children after she and her wife divorced in 2007. At the time, she was not open about her gender identity. Two years later, Lynn decided to socially transition. She and her ex-wife agreed that their children should live with Lynn's ex-wife. The boys would move back in with Lynn when her transition was complete. However, Lynn's ex-wife petitioned a Texas court for full custody

SEX CRIMINALS

Until the 1960s, all 50 states enforced sodomy laws. In general terms, sodomy refers to any type of sexual intercourse that does not result in procreation. Although laws in some states also applied to heterosexual people, during and after the 1960s they were generally used to criminalize gays and lesbians. They have been used as justification for denying LGBTQ people employment, protection from hate crimes, and the ability to adopt or foster a child. The US Supreme Court ruled that such laws were unconstitutional in 2003 in the case *Lawrence v. Texas*. This ruling states that a person has a right to privacy in their own home. Though 12 states still have anti-sodomy laws on the books, the laws are not technically enforceable as long as *Lawrence v. Texas* remains the precedent.

of their youngest son. Lynn's parental rights were terminated because of what the court called her "dangerous lifestyle": being transgender. Her name was removed from her son's birth certificate. She is not allowed to contact him until he is an adult.[3]

Some instances of courtroom discrimination have even graver consequences. In 1993, Charles Rhines was convicted of murdering an employee in a South Dakota doughnut shop. The jury sentenced him to death. Years later, interviews with former jury members indicated Rhines's sexual orientation impacted his sentence. Some jurors were disgusted by Rhines's homosexuality. According to advocates for Rhines, evidence "suggests that at least some members of the jury accepted the notion that life in prison without parole would be fun for a gay person."[4] To make sure he did not enjoy his punishment, they voted for the death penalty. Rhines appealed the decision in 2017. Both the state and the US Supreme Court refused to reopen the case. The state said evidence of discrimination was misinterpreted by Rhines's defense attorneys.

DISCRIMINATION IN CORRECTIONAL FACILITIES

LGBTQ people also face discriminatory treatment in correctional facilities such as jails, prisons, and juvenile detention centers.

One example is the use of solitary confinement as punishment. According to a 2015 report by the Bureau of Justice Statistics, 28 percent of nonheterosexual people in prison had been put in solitary confinement in the previous year. Only 18 percent of heterosexual prisoners were sent to solitary confinement.[5] LGBTQ people also face harsher treatment by guards, staff, and other prisoners. This includes verbal harassment, physical and sexual abuse, and inadequate access to health care.

Trans prisoners face even greater barriers. Many correctional institutions assign inmates to facilities based on the sex marker on their birth certificates. That means trans women and girls are forced to stay in men's prisons or juvenile correctional facilities. Trans men and boys are put in women's prisons or juvenile correctional facilities. This not only disregards and belittles trans people but also places them at higher risk for harassment and assault.

COURT CHANGES ALARM LGBTQ ADVOCATES

Unless Congress amends current legislation, it will be up to the nine justices of the US Supreme Court to determine the legality of LGBTQ discrimination in education, housing, and employment. Recent turnover in the Supreme Court has made many LGBTQ advocates nervous about the prospective outcomes. Between 2017 and 2018, President Trump appointed two conservative justices, Neil Gorsuch and Brett Kavanaugh. Many LGBTQ people and allies fear the new justices will take a narrower view of illegal discrimination, thereby resulting in the suppression of LGBTQ civil rights.

Inmates in jails and prisons are usually separated by gender. Some prisons only house inmates of one gender.

Many facilities also prevent trans people from accessing proper medical care. For example, Jessica Hicklin was an inmate at Potosi Correctional Center (PCC) in Mineral Point, Missouri. Until 2018, a Missouri Department of Corrections (MDOC) policy banned HRT for inmates who were not taking HRT before incarceration. Hicklin was diagnosed with gender dysphoria while at PCC but was not allowed to follow her doctors' recommendations for HRT and body-hair removal. She could not purchase gender-affirming products at the canteen,

NEW GUIDANCE PROTECTS RELIGIOUS FREEDOMS

In 2016, four female inmates in Texas sued the federal government over the *Transgender Offender Manual*'s instruction to place trans inmates in facilities that match their gender identity. They argued that sharing facilities with trans women "violate[d] their constitutional rights and their rights under the Religious Freedom Restoration Act."[6] Only two of the women lived in a facility that had any trans prisoners, and those prisoners were in different housing units. Still, the court ruled in the women's favor. That put in motion the changes to the 2018 edition of the manual, which now states its purpose is to "ensure the Bureau of Prisons properly identifies, tracks, and provides services to the transgender population, consistent with maintaining security and good order in Federal prisons."[7]

such as women's shampoo or makeup. In May 2018, a federal district court ordered that MDOC and its contracted health-care provider allow Hicklin access to HRT and other transition-related care.

WHERE WE ARE

Members of the LGBTQ community have few protections when it comes to discrimination within the criminal justice system. There are no federal or state laws that dictate how they should be treated during interactions with police, in court, or in prison. In 2012, the Federal Bureau of Prisons (BOP) under the Obama administration issued guidance that instructed all correctional facilities to house inmates based on their gender identity. Since the *Transgender Offender Manual* was not a law, several facilities ignored the instructions. Yet LGBTQ civil rights activists viewed the directive as a step in the right direction.

Those gains were erased in May 2018. The BOP issued a new version of the manual. It says federal correctional facilities must "use biological sex as the initial determination" for where a prisoner is placed. Gender identity will only be considered in "rare cases."[8] Activists see this as a blow to the health and safety of trans people serving jail time, 35 percent of whom have experienced sexual assault while incarcerated. This percentage is much higher compared with the 4 percent of the general prison population who have reported sexual assault. "My concern about this is that it is going to directly place transgender people in harm's way," says Megan McLemore of Human Rights Watch. "This is something that is going to result in harm and death."[9] Despite the setback, LGBTQ advocacy groups continue to petition for equal and fair treatment for all people, no matter their orientation or identity.

DISCUSSION STARTERS

- Should a parent's sexual orientation or gender identity have an impact on their parental rights? Why or why not?

- How do personal prejudice and bias impact the criminal justice system? What could be done to change that?

- Do you think it is important for trans people to be placed in prisons that align with their gender identities? Why or why not?

People who experience discrimination may feel increased stress. This can lead to negative health outcomes.

EFFECTS OF DISCRIMINATION

B eing the target of discrimination is not a small inconvenience. For many people, discrimination is a constant source of pain, frustration, and indignity. It also has long-term side effects that can negatively affect one's future. At the root of these problems is stress. A 2016 American Psychological Association (APA) report points out that people who constantly deal with discrimination are always in "a state of heightened vigilance."[1] They worry about what they say, where they go, and how they appear to others. These high-alert behaviors trigger even more stress. It is a never-ending cycle that affects one's physical, mental, social, and financial well-being.

SOURCES OF STRESS

In addition to worrying about discrimination outside the home, some LGBTQ people may also have to worry about discrimination from close family and friends. In a 2012 survey of 13- to 17-year-old LGBTQ youths by the HRC, 26 percent of

respondents said the biggest problem in their lives was having a family who did not accept them for who they are. Another 18 percent identified fear of being out or open about their sexuality or gender identity as their biggest obstacle.[2]

How family members respond to someone after they come out has an enormous impact on that person's life. Susan Kuklin's 2014 book, *Beyond Magenta: Transgender Teens Speak Out*, shares the stories of six teenagers who identify as trans, nonbinary, or genderqueer. Some of the teens had familial support. That was the case for Cameron, who links the support of their family to the relative ease of coming out to others: "If my parents weren't supporting me, most of the teachers wouldn't have listened."[3]

LGBTQ YOUTUBE CENSORSHIP

It can be hard for teens in some parts of the country to make connections within the LGBTQ community. Perhaps there are not LGBTQ-friendly resources available, or maybe they do not feel comfortable learning about gender identity and sexual orientation in public. For these people, YouTube has been an invaluable source of information and connections within the LGBTQ community.

The once-positive relationship between YouTube and the LGBTQ community soured in 2017. Prominent LGBTQ content providers, including Rowan Ellis and Tyler Oakley, noticed some of their videos were blocked by the company's content filters. These filters are generally used to hide explicit material. Instead, they were blocking every video that mentioned same-sex romantic partners or LGBTQ issues. YouTube officials apologized, but the problems persisted into 2019. This censorship makes it even harder for teens who are searching for support or information to find supportive communities. It also penalizes LGBTQ YouTubers, many of whom earn money based on the number of times their videos are viewed.

However, Nat had no family support when they tried to tell their family they were not a girl. Their parents took away their computer, cell phone, and books. They were only allowed to leave the house for school. Nat grew depressed and despondent. They attempted suicide twice. After high school, Nat cut off most contact with their family. "I needed to get out of the environment that was making me feel bad about myself," Nat told Kuklin.[4]

FAMILY REJECTION AND HOMELESSNESS

According to a 2012 Williams Institute study, up to 40 percent of youths experiencing homelessness are LGBTQ youths. This is largely because of family rejection. Experts estimate that as many as 50 percent of LGBTQ teens have negative experiences when they come out to their families. More than 25 percent are kicked out of their homes. If they do not have friends or other family members on which they can rely, these youths may end up in shelters or on the streets.[5]

PERSONAL EFFECTS OF DISCRIMINATION

The chronic stress of familial and societal rejection can negatively impact all aspects of a person's life, starting with physical health. In the APA study, people who reported extreme levels of stress were twice as likely to report "fair" or "poor" health compared with those who reported low stress levels.

THE INVISIBLE MAJORITY

Bisexual people are sexually attracted to people of their same gender and people of other genders. They account for 52 percent of the LGBTQ community.[6] Yet despite their numbers, they generally face more discrimination than their gay and lesbian peers. Nearly two-thirds of bisexual people have experienced discrimination or harassment at work because of their sexual orientation. More than 60 percent of bisexual women and 37 percent of bisexual men have been the victims of violence or aggressive behaviors. They are also more likely to experience anxiety and depression at higher rates than heterosexuals, lesbians, and gay men.[7]

The problem is that bisexuality is often seen as not being a "real" sexual orientation. Some people incorrectly think it is an experimental phase. Others claim it is a "pit stop" on the way to identifying as gay. Neither of those things is necessarily true. Bisexual people continue to be bisexual regardless of the gender of their current partner.

Ignorance about bisexuality and those who identify with it has caused what many people call the erasure of the bisexual community. When people aren't seen and heard, their needs can't be met. That's why bisexual people have higher rates of anxiety, depression, and other mood disorders than heterosexual people and gay men and lesbians. They have higher rates of heart disease and cancer risk factors and lower rates of cancer screenings than their heterosexual counterparts. Public education and positive media representation are the first steps to changing these problems.

The bisexual pride flag is pink, purple, and blue.

Other studies have linked stress to higher occurrences of digestive problems, headaches, high blood pressure, diabetes, obesity, and even viral infections such as the common cold.

Medical experts think the culprit may be the hormone cortisol. Cortisol is released when a person encounters a stressful situation. It increases sugars in the bloodstream and alters the immune system. It also suppresses the digestive system, reproductive system, and growth. In most cases, cortisol levels go back to normal when stressors are gone. But for people who are always stressed, cortisol levels remain high. That can lead to illness and physical problems.

Increased levels of cortisol can also impact one's mental health. Combined with other factors, such as feelings of shame, despair, or low self-esteem, it can lead to depression and anxiety. The 2016 US Youth Risk Behavior Survey indicated that the 8 percent of students who identified as nonheterosexual experienced higher rates of depression than their heterosexual peers.[8] They were also more likely to engage in self-destructive behaviors, such as suicide and self-harm. Some people try to cope with feelings of anxiety and despair by using alcohol, tobacco, and other addictive substances. Those can also cause long-term health problems.

Decreased physical and mental health impacts every aspect of a person's life. People who don't feel well are less likely to

AVERAGE STRESS LEVELS IN THE UNITED STATES[9]

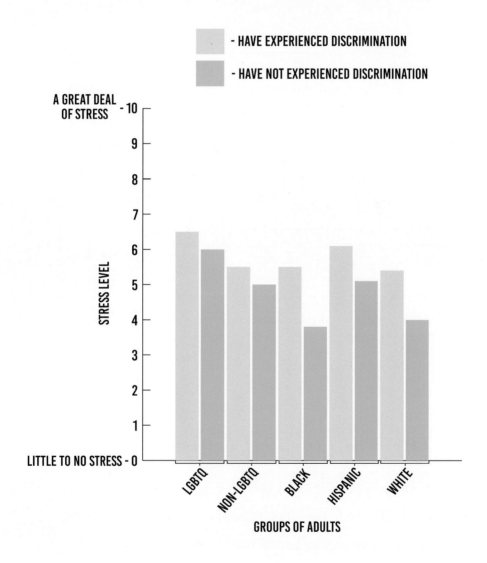

- HAVE EXPERIENCED DISCRIMINATION

- HAVE NOT EXPERIENCED DISCRIMINATION

A GREAT DEAL OF STRESS - 10

STRESS LEVEL

LITTLE TO NO STRESS - 0

LGBTQ · NON-LGBTQ · BLACK · HISPANIC · WHITE

GROUPS OF ADULTS

According to the American Psychological Association, the average stress level in the United States is 5.1.

go to school and work, especially if they have to endure harassment and discrimination in those places. Frequent school absences lead to poorer grades. Low grades ultimately lower one's prospects for a successful, financially stable career. The amount of money a person makes affects their ability to afford housing, medical care, and basic necessities. What happens to someone as a teen or young adult has a lasting impact on their future.

THE PUBLIC PRICE OF DISCRIMINATION

Anti-LGBTQ discrimination affects everyone, not just those who identify as members of the LGBTQ community. According to the World Economic Forum, a Switzerland-based nonprofit organization dedicated to understanding and shaping global business, discrimination stifles innovation. When a person is denied educational and career opportunities because of who they are, the rest of the world misses out on their ideas and contributions.

Therefore, countries that allow discrimination against minority groups produce fewer new products, services, and business ideas.

That has a major negative impact on national economies. A 2014 study by the World Bank concluded that India, the second-most-populous country in the world, could be losing as much as $32 billion per year because of anti-LGBTQ policies and acts of discrimination. In other words, if LGBTQ people in India were allowed the same opportunities as heterosexual, cisgender people, the country's economy would be $32 billion richer.[10]

Economic growth means higher average incomes and lower unemployment rates. When people make more money, they pay more in taxes. Tax money is used for public services, such as education, law enforcement, health care, and national infrastructure. Improvements in those areas benefit everyone.

LGBTQ-FRIENDLY EMPLOYERS

Some of the nation's top employers have made it a priority to hire LGBTQ employees. Employment site Glassdoor lists Uber, Google, IKEA, Microsoft, PayPal, Coca-Cola, Gap, Target, and Apple among the top 20 major LGBTQ-friendly employers.[11] Its rankings are based on company policies, including antidiscrimination policies and insurance coverage, and employee feedback.

Businesses in North Carolina posted signs near their restrooms in support of the LGBTQ community.

When countries, states, cities, and companies implement policies that make it difficult for LGBTQ people to contribute to the economy, cisgender and heterosexual people suffer too.

Innovation and economic growth are more likely to take place in areas where minorities are welcome. Places that discriminate against certain groups, such as the LGBTQ community, lose their competitive advantage. People do not want to move there for jobs. Those who are already there relocate to more accepting parts of the country. For example, in 2016 the North Carolina state legislature passed House Bill 2 (HB2), otherwise known as the "bathroom bill." It required people to use restrooms in government buildings that matched the gender on their birth certificates and prevented cities from passing laws that protect the LGBTQ community from discrimination. Because of that, PayPal scrapped its plans to expand its offices in Charlotte, North Carolina. Experts estimate that this decision cost the state $2.66 billion and more than 400 new jobs.[12] Even after the North Carolina state legislature replaced HB2 with HB142, which removed language pertaining to bathroom usage, PayPal remained uninterested in bringing more business to North Carolina.

DISCUSSION STARTERS

- What other stressors do LGBTQ teens and adults face? How could they be prevented?

- How are you affected by stress? Where do you experience stress in your daily life?

9

FIGHTING AGAINST DISCRIMINATION

A cceptance of the LGBTQ community has increased dramatically since the end of the 1900s. But there is still a long way to go in securing equality and fair treatment for people of all sexual orientations and gender identities. Leading the way are a host of LGBTQ-focused civil rights organizations dedicated to ending discrimination in education, employment, health care, and the law.

ORGANIZATIONS TO WATCH

With more than three million members, the HRC is the largest LGBTQ civil rights organization in the United States. Its mission is to "end discrimination against LGBTQ people and realize a world that achieves fundamental fairness and equality for all."[1] The organization endorses LGBTQ-friendly politicians and organizes social media campaigns related to current events and

In 2018, the HRC endorsed Arizona Senate candidate Kyrsten Sinema. Sinema won the election.

national policy. For nearly a decade, HRC championed marriage equality at the state and national levels. It was one of the leading organizers of efforts to bring marriage equality before the Supreme Court in 2015. It also played a part in the repeal of the military's DADT policy in 2010. HRC also holds corporations, health-care providers, cities, and states accountable for their treatment of LGBTQ populations in its annual index reports.

Lambda Legal is also dedicated to securing civil rights for LGBTQ people, as well as those who are living with HIV. It does this by educating the public, working to change public policy, and providing legal representation for people who have faced discrimination because of their sexual orientation, gender identity, or HIV status. In the past several years, Lambda Legal has represented many discrimination cases brought forth by LGBTQ people. In addition to employment, family, education, and health-care cases, Lambda Legal also has LGBTQ clients facing issues with immigration, police and criminal justice, and religious exemptions.

The Transgender Law Center is also a nonprofit legal organization. Its goal is to ensure "that all people can live safely, authentically, and free from discrimination regardless of their gender identity or expression."[2] It does this by providing legal guidance and advice, connecting trans plaintiffs to legal services, and advocating for changes in public policy and law. Its primary focus is economic justice and health-care access for trans and gender-nonconforming people.

HRC'S EQUALITY INDEXES

The HRC keeps close track of how LGBTQ people are treated in the world at large. Every year, it publishes four indexes that rank various entities with respect to how they treat LGBTQ people. The Corporate Equality Index rates employers' nondiscrimination policies. The Healthcare Equality Index looks at how well health-care facilities care for LGBTQ patients. The Municipal Quality Index looks at the inclusivity of towns and cities. The State Equality Index examines state LGBTQ policies. Each report is available for public review on the HRC's website.

LGBTQ REPRESENTATION ON-SCREEN

Dozens of television shows and movies, including *Will & Grace*, *Glee*, *Modern Family*, *Pose*, *Brokeback Mountain*, *Boys Don't Cry*, and *Moonlight*, have shown a variety of experiences within the LGBTQ community. These types of productions are important in decreasing anti-LGBTQ stigma while making the community's stories more visible. However, GLAAD indicates there is more work to be done. According to the organization's preview of the 2018–2019 television season, 8.8 percent of regular, or frequently appearing, characters scheduled to appear on scripted broadcast shows could be classified as LGBTQ. Although this is the highest percentage of LGBTQ representation in television history, GLAAD is pushing TV studios to bring that number up to 10 percent by 2021.[3]

GLAAD's 2017 Studio Responsibility Index, which tracks representation in film, showed that nearly 13 percent of major studio movies had an LGBTQ character. However, 50 percent of movies with an LGBTQ character gave those characters "less than five minutes of screen time."[4] Additionally, most of the characters were gay men.

Representation matters. Telling LGBTQ stories not only educates the public but also validates the experiences of those within the LGBTQ community. It is an important step in ending the prejudice that leads to discrimination.

In 2019, trans actress Nicole Maines became the first trans person to play a superhero on TV. Maines plays Nia Nal on *Supergirl*.

It also works in the areas of school safety, immigration, and the criminal justice system. In November 2018, it brought a civil case against the state of New Mexico after the death of Roxsana Hernandez, a trans Honduran asylum seeker.

There are also several professional organizations advocating for LGBTQ rights in the United States. GLSEN works to improve educational experiences for LGBTQ K–12 students. It educates teachers and administrators about the needs of LGBTQ students and advocates for changes to public education policies. It is also the center of the national network of GSAs.

The Gay and Lesbian Medical Association is an organization of LGBTQ health-care professionals. Its mission is to ensure equity and equality for LGBTQ health-care providers and their patients.

Out & Equal advocates for workplace equality around the world. In addition to offering training and guidance for

LGBTQ-ONLY SOCIAL NETWORKING

Social media can be a great tool for connecting with other people. It can also be a platform for spreading hate. That is why some LGBTQ people prefer apps and social media networks designed specifically for them. One of those is Moovz. Started in 2014, Moovz is a social media and dating site hybrid. Its main component is a downloadable app for adults aged 18 and older. It also has an all-ages news and opinion site, On the Moovz, that is open to the public.

major companies and government agencies, it also provides networking opportunities for LGBTQ employees.

SOCIAL MEDIA MOVEMENTS

The widespread use of social media has changed the way people learn about and join social movements. With a few keystrokes, people around the globe come together to share stories and advocate for change. One of the earliest of these movements was the It Gets Better Project. In 2010, advice columnist and author Dan Savage and his partner, Terry Miller, posted a video to YouTube. In it, they described the discrimination they faced as teens for being gay. They assured viewers, "However bad it is now, it gets better."[5] Savage promoted the YouTube page in his nationally syndicated column. Soon, other adults were sharing their messages of hope and support for the next generation of LGBTQ teenagers. Today, more than 60,000 people have shared their stories.[6]

Another viral social media campaign, Coming Out Matters, launched in 2014. Led by celebrity ambassador Jonny Drubel of the E! show *Rich Kids of Beverly Hills*, it aimed to decrease the fear of coming out within the LGBTQ community and help those who struggle to do so. People shared their coming-out stories in videos and typed messages. Although the campaign is no longer active, the hashtag #ComingOutMatters still appears on Twitter and other social media platforms.

In response to a Trump administration ban on transgender servicepeople, LGBTQ people and their allies held a rally in New York City.

LGBTQ people and their allies also take to social media to speak out against limiting laws and policies. In October 2018, the *New York Times* reported that the Trump administration was considering changing the legal definition of *gender*. Within hours, trans people and their supporters began voicing their dissent on the internet with the hashtags #WeWillNotBeErased and #WontBeErased. Messages were accompanied by personal photos. Within days, trans activists and allies held rallies across the nation. At a rally in Saint Petersburg, Florida, speaker Taylor TeMonet Burts addressed the Trump administration: "Your pencil is not big enough to erase us. People are people. We deserve respect."[7]

ORIGINS OF A RALLYING CRY

The phrase "We will not be erased" originated with a May 31, 2017, Instagram post by actress Laverne Cox to commemorate the annual Trans Day of Visibility. Trans activist Chelsea Manning used similar words in July 2017 in a *New York Times* op-ed about President Trump's proposed ban of trans people in the military. At the end of the year, the HRC projected the words "We will not be erased" onto a Trump hotel in Washington, DC.[8] It was a response to the Trump administration's prohibition of using the word *transgender* in official Centers for Disease Control and Prevention budget documents.

HOPE FOR THE FUTURE

Eradicating anti-LGBTQ discrimination in the United States is not easy. There is a lot of work to be done to decrease stigma.

SENATOR ORRIN HATCH

Liberal-leaning news and opinion outlets have long argued for an end to LGBTQ prejudice and discrimination. Yet perhaps the most significant endorsement for change is one from the opposite side of the political aisle. In December 2018, Republican Senator Orrin Hatch of Utah gave his farewell speech after 42 years in the US Senate. Hatch, a conservative Christian and Mormon, spent part of his speech encouraging his fellow conservatives and Republicans to find a balance between honoring religious liberty and protecting the rights of the LGBTQ community. "I believe we can find substantial common ground on these issues that will enable us to both safeguard the ability of religious individuals to live their faith and protect LGBTQ individuals from . . . discrimination," Hatch said.[10]

There are laws to be amended and policies to be updated. Yet LGBTQ civil rights activists agree that hope is on the horizon for younger generations. People born anytime after 1996 have noticeably rejected traditional notions of sexual orientation and gender identity. They are not as restricted by gender roles as previous generations were. They also are less likely to identify as heterosexual. According to a 2016 study by trend forecasting agency J. Walter Thompson Innovation Group, only 48 percent of people between 13 and 20 years old identify as being "exclusively heterosexual."[9] These people are also redefining what it means to accept and support people who fall outside the cisgender, heterosexual norm.

For minority groups in the United States, the path to equal rights has historically been a long and bumpy road. The LGBTQ community's experience is no different. In a span of just five years, it saw both great progress, such as the legalization of same-sex marriage, and troubling lows, such as the Trump administration's push to redefine the term *gender*. While this is frustrating for many advocates and allies, it is also normal. Changing minds and hearts takes time. Those leading the movement for LGBTQ civil rights encourage everyone—gay or straight, cis or trans—to make their voices heard. In his 2018 farewell letter to the advocacy organization Human Rights Watch, former LGBT Advocacy Director Boris Dittrich reminded members of the LGBTQ community and their allies to stay positive. "The future is not in front of us, it's inside of us," he wrote.[11]

DISCUSSION STARTERS

- Have you ever used a hashtag for solidarity on social media? What was the hashtag?

- How might discrimination change in the next five years? The next ten years?

ESSENTIAL FACTS

SIGNIFICANT EVENTS

- In 1964, Congress passed the Equal Rights Act. It included the Fair Housing Act, which prevented housing discrimination, and Title VII, which prevented employment discrimination. Since then, lawmakers, judges, plaintiffs, and defendants have debated the meaning of the word *sex* as it is used in laws opposing LGBTQ discrimination.

- In 2017, President Donald Trump's administration began rolling back protections for LGBTQ people. This included issuing an order to ban trans people from military service and an assertion that LGBTQ people were not protected from employment discrimination. That same year, the Trump administration removed Obama-era protections that allowed trans people to use school restrooms and locker rooms that match their gender identity. In 2018, the Trump administration proposed changing the definition of *gender* to refer only to biological sex.

- In 2017 and 2018, two US district appellate courts ruled that employment discrimination based on sexual orientation was illegal.

KEY PLAYERS

- The late Donald Zarda was a skydiving instructor who lost his job after coming out to one of his clients. The US Court of Appeals of the Second Circuit ruled in his favor in 2018. His former employer is trying to bring the case to the US Supreme Court.

- Martha Wetzel was discriminated against at her retirement community for being a lesbian. A court ruled that it was the facility's responsibility to protect her from harassment.

- The Human Rights Campaign (HRC) is the largest LGBTQ civil rights organization in the United States. It was a major player in the push for legalizing same-sex marriage in 2015.

- Lambda Legal is a nonprofit legal organization that helps LGBTQ people and people living with HIV fight back against discrimination. Over the years it has represented hundreds of plaintiffs whose rights have been violated, including Drew Adams, Jameka Evans, Kimberly Hively, and Jack Zawadski.

IMPACT ON SOCIETY

Discrimination impacts members of the LGBTQ community in every aspect of their lives, from health to education to employment. Federal law offers no explicit protections against discrimination based on a person's sexual orientation or gender identity. Courts don't agree on whether such rights exist. The continuation of LGBTQ discrimination doesn't just hurt the health and livelihood of LGBTQ people; it hurts the economic and social growth of society as a whole.

QUOTE

"[Doctors] do not understand my body. So why would I trust them to help me with my health and wellness?"

— *Sinclair Sexsmith,* The Remedy: Queer and Trans Voices on Health and Health Care

GLOSSARY

BIAS
Prejudice in favor of or against one thing, person, or group compared with another, usually in a way considered to be unfair.

DEFENDANT
A person accused of a crime who has had a legal charge made against them.

EQUITY
Justice in the way people are treated, which does not mean treating people the same.

GENDER DYSPHORIA
The distress caused by having a gender identity that does not match the sex assigned at birth.

GENDER EXPRESSION
The outward appearance of someone's gender identity.

GENDER IDENTITY
A person's perception of their gender, which may or may not correspond with the sex they were assigned at birth.

HORMONE REPLACEMENT THERAPY (HRT)
A drug regimen for some trans people that introduces estrogen or testosterone into the body to change its appearance.

IDEOLOGY
A set of ideas and beliefs of a group.

INCARCERATION
The state of being in prison.

MISGENDER
To refer to someone with a word (such as a pronoun) that does not accurately reflect their gender identity.

NONBINARY
Having a gender identity that is neither male nor female, or sometimes both male and female.

PLAINTIFF
The one accusing a defendant in a court of law.

PRECEDENT
In court cases, a ruling on a case that serves as a guide for future related rulings.

STIGMA
A set of negative and often unfair beliefs that a society or group of people has about something.

ADDITIONAL RESOURCES

SELECTED BIBLIOGRAPHY

Haag, Matthew. "LGBT Students in Oregon Were Bullied and Forced to Read Bible, Report Says." *New York Times*, 16 May 2018, nytimes.com. Accessed 14 Jan. 2019.

"The Rights of Lesbian, Gay, Bisexual, and Transgender People." *ACLU*, 2018, aclu.org. Accessed 14 Jan. 2019.

Tortelli, Brett. "The Fear and Discrimination in LGBT Healthcare." *Institute for Public Health*, 14 Sept. 2016, publichealth.wustl.edu. Accessed 14 Jan. 2019.

FURTHER READINGS

Harris, Duchess, and Martha Lundin. *LGBTQ Rights and the Law*. Abdo, 2020.

Jacobs, Thomas A. *What Are My Rights? Q&A about Teens and the Law*. 4th ed. Free Spirit Publishing, 2019.

ONLINE RESOURCES

To learn more about LGBTQ discrimination, please visit **abdobooklinks.com** or scan this QR code. These links are routinely monitored and updated to provide the most current information available.

MORE INFORMATION

For more information on this subject, contact or visit the following organizations:

AMERICAN CIVIL LIBERTIES UNION

125 Broad St., Eighteenth Floor
New York, NY 10004
aclu.org

The American Civil Liberties Union (ACLU) is a nonprofit organization dedicated to defending and preserving the individual rights of all Americans.

CENTER FOR AMERICAN PROGRESS

1333 H St. NW, Tenth Floor
Washington, DC 20005
americanprogress.org

The Center for American Progress is an independent, nonpartisan policy institute with progressive ideals. It aims to shape policies regarding education, LGBTQ issues, immigration, and poverty through public action and media coverage.

GLAAD

5455 Wilshire Blvd., Suite 1500
Los Angeles, CA 90036
glaad.org

Formerly known as the Gay and Lesbian Alliance against Defamation, GLAAD monitors media coverage of the LGBTQ community. It challenges unfair, biased reporting and pushes media organizations for more representative coverage of LGBTQ people.

SOURCE NOTES

CHAPTER 1. A HOSTILE ATMOSPHERE

1. Kate Briquelet. "School Banned Gay Prom Dates: Lawsuit." *Daily Beast*, 12 May 2017, thedailybeast.com. Accessed 19 Mar. 2019.

2. "Student Sues Buffalo School District, Homophobic Principal for Denying Gay Straight Alliance." *OutSmart*, 11 May 2017, outsmartmagazine.com. Accessed 19 Mar. 2019.

3. "Student Sues Buffalo School District."

4. Sandhya Somashekhar. "They Lived as a Gay Couple in Mississippi for 20 Years. The Worst Indignity Came in Death, Lawsuit Says." *Washington Post*, 4 May 2017, washingtonpost.com. Accessed 19 Mar. 2019.

5. Samantha Allen. "Harvard Study: LGBT People of Color Suffer Double Discrimination." *Daily Beast*, 28 Nov. 2017, thedailybeast.com. Accessed 19 Mar. 2019.

6. American Psychological Association. "Stress in America: The Impact of Discrimination." *Stress in America Survey*, 2016, apa.org. Accessed 19 Mar. 2019.

CHAPTER 2. POLITICAL FRAMEWORK

1. "Discrimination in America: Experiences and Views of LGBTQ Americans." *NPR, Robert Wood Johnson Foundation, and Harvard T.H. Chan School of Public Health*, Nov. 2017, npr.org. Accessed 19 Mar. 2019.

2. Movement Advancement Project. "Non-Discrimination Laws." *Movement Advancement Project*, 18 Mar. 2019, lgbtmap.org. Accessed 19 Mar. 2019.

3. Movement Advancement Project. "Local Non-Discrimination Ordinances." *Movement Advancement Project*, 18 Mar. 2019, lgbtmap.org. Accessed 19 Mar. 2019.

4. German Lopez. "Why You Shouldn't Freak Out about the Masterpiece Cakeshop Ruling." *Vox*, 4 June 2018, vox.com. Accessed 19 Mar. 2019.

5. Movement Advancement Project. "Religious Exemption Laws." *Movement Advancement Project*, 18 Mar. 2019, lgbtmap.org. Accessed 19 Mar. 2019.

6. "Results 2018." *Victory Fund*, 2018, victoryfund.org. Accessed 19 Mar. 2019.

7. Hunter Woodall and Lynn Horsley. "GOP Official on Davids: Radical Socialist, Lesbian Will Be Sent Back to Reservation." *Kansas City Star*, 9 Oct. 2018, kansascity.com. Accessed 19 Mar. 2019.

8. Brianna Heldt. "Leaked HHS Memo Reveals a Move to Identify People's Gender on a Biological Basis." *Townhall*, 23 Oct. 2018, townhall.com. Accessed 19 Mar. 2019.

9. Julie Moreau. "Advocacy Groups, Political Organizations Go After the LGBTQ Vote." *NBC News*, 12 Sept. 2018, nbcnews.com. Accessed 19 Mar. 2019.

10. Moreau, "Advocacy Groups, Political Organizations."

11. Erica L. Green et al. "'Transgender' Could Be Defined Out of Existence under Trump Administration." *New York Times*, 21 Oct. 2018, nytimes.com. Accessed 19 Mar. 2019.

12. Green et al., "'Transgender' Could Be Defined Out of Existence."

CHAPTER 3. EMPLOYMENT

1. "Know Your Rights: Title VII of the Civil Rights Act of 1964." *American Association of University Women*, 2018, aauw.org. Accessed 19 Mar. 2019.

2. "2017 Workplace Equality Fact Sheet." *Out & Equal*, n.d., outandequal.org. Accessed 19 Mar. 2019.

3. Joe Pinsker. "Unequal Pay: The Gay Wage Gap." *Atlantic*, 17 June 2015, theatlantic.com. Accessed 19 Mar. 2019.

4. Lambda Legal. "Evans v. Georgia Regional Hospital." *Lambda Legal*, n.d., lambdalegal.org. Accessed 19 Mar. 2019.

5. Kari Paul. "It's National Coming Out Day—But Nearly 50% of LGBTQ Americans Are in the Closet at Work." *MarketWatch*, 11 Oct. 2018, marketwatch.com. Accessed 19 Mar. 2019.

6. Lila Shapiro. "Boss Who Asked Transgender Woman 'What Are You?' Agrees to Significant Settlement." *HuffPost*, 10 Sept. 2015, huffingtonpost.com. Accessed 19 Mar. 2019.

7. Richard Wolf. "Supreme Court Won't Hear LGBT Job Discrimination Case." *USA Today*, 11 Dec. 2017, usatoday.com. Accessed 19 Mar. 2019.

8. Vanessa Chesnut. "Plaintiff at Center of Landmark Gay-Rights Case Never Got to Witness His Victory." *NBC News*, 3 Mar. 2018, nbcnews.com. Accessed 19 Mar. 2019.

CHAPTER 4. HEALTH CARE

1. "Discrimination in America: Experiences and Views of LGBTQ Americans." *NPR, Robert Wood Johnson Foundation, and Harvard T.H. Chan School of Public Health*, Nov. 2017, npr.org. Accessed 19 Mar. 2019.

2. "The Report of the 2015 US Transgender Survey." *National Center for Transgender Equality*, Dec. 2016, transequality.org. Accessed 19 Mar. 2019.

3. Zena Sharman. *The Remedy: Queer and Trans Voices on Health and Health Care*. Arsenal Pulp, 2016. 73.

4. Phil McCausland. "CVS Apologizes for Pharmacist Who Refused to Fill Transgender Woman's Prescription." *NBC News*, 21 July 2018, nbcnews.com. Accessed 19 Mar. 2019.

5. Brett Tortelli. "The Fear of Discrimination in LGBT Healthcare." *Washington University in St. Louis Institute for Public Health*, 14 Sept. 2016, publichealth.wustl.edu. Accessed 19 Mar. 2019.

6. "Discrimination in America: Experiences and Views of LGBTQ Americans."

7. Bill Browning. "Doctor Refuses to Treat 6-Day-Old Baby Because Her Parents Are Lesbians." *LGBTQ Nation*, 25 Apr. 2018, lgbtqnation.com. Accessed 19 Mar. 2019.

8. "Michigan." *Beyond I Do*, n.d., beyondido.org. Accessed 19 Mar. 2019.

9. Ryan Thoreson. "'You Don't Want Second Best': Anti-LGBT Discrimination in US Health Care." *Human Rights Watch*, n.d., hrw.org. Accessed 19 Mar. 2019.

10. Sean Cahill. "LGBT Community and People with HIV Have Much to Lose in Health Debate." *The Hill*, 8 Mar. 2017, thehill.com. Accessed 19 Mar. 2019.

11. Donald G. McNeil Jr. "He Took a Drug to Prevent AIDS. Then He Couldn't Get Disability Insurance." *New York Times*, 12 Feb. 2018, nytimes.com. Accessed 19 Mar. 2019.

12. BBC News. "US FDA Partially Lifts Gay Men Blood Donation Ban." *BBC News*, 22 Dec. 2015, bbc.com. Accessed 19 Mar. 2019.

CHAPTER 5. EDUCATION

1. Jillian Ward. "North Bend School District Faces Discrimination Claims after LGBT Students Allegedly Forced to Read Bible for Punishment." *News-Review*, 10 May 2018, nrtoday.com. Accessed 19 Mar. 2019.

2. Ward, "North Bend School District Faces Discrimination Claims."

3. Ryan Hass. "Southern Oregon School District Settles over LGBTQ Discrimination." *Oregon Public Broadcasting*, 21 May 2018, opb.org. Accessed 19 Mar. 2019.

4. "2017 National School Climate Survey." *GLSEN*, 2018, glsen.org. Accessed 19 Mar. 2019.

5. "2017 National School Climate Survey."

6. Drew Adams. "My High School Won't Let Me Use the Bathroom, So I'm Suing It." *Lambda Legal*, 28 June 2017, lambdalegal.org. Accessed 19 Mar. 2019.

7. "Preventing Harassment and Protecting Free Speech at School." *ACLU*, n.d., aclu.org. Accessed 19 Mar. 2019.

8. "2017 National School Climate Survey."

9. Rebecca Klein. "These Schools Get Millions of Tax Dollars to Discriminate against LGBTQ Students." *HuffPost*, 16 Dec. 2017, huffingtonpost.com. Accessed 19 Mar. 2019.

SOURCE NOTES
CONTINUED

10. Klein, "These Schools Get Millions of Tax Dollars."

11. Clifford Rosky. "Anti-Gay Curriculum Laws." *Columbia Law Review*, vol. 117, no. 6, n.d., columbialawreview.org. Accessed 19 Mar. 2019.

CHAPTER 6. HOUSING

1. "North Carolina." *Beyond I Do*, n.d., beyondido.org. Accessed 19 Mar. 2019.

2. Skylar Herron. "Transitioning While Homeless: Skylar's Story." *Trans Equality Now!*, 14 Mar. 2018, medium.com. Accessed 19 Mar. 2019.

3. Richard Eisenberg. "Housing Discrimination: The Next Hurdle for LGBT Couples." *Forbes*, 2 July 2015, forbes.com. Accessed 19 Mar. 2019.

4. Diane K. Levy. "Discrimination Is Limiting LGBTQ People's Access to Rental Housing." *Urban Wire*, 2 Aug. 2017, urban.org. Accessed 19 Mar. 2019.

5. Levy, "Discrimination Is Limiting LGBTQ People's Access to Rental Housing."

6. Meagan Flynn. "Can Airbnb Fix Its Discrimination Problem? Gay Houston Man Denied Housing Says No." *Houston Press*, 13 July 2016, houstonpress.com. Accessed 19 Mar. 2019.

7. Airbnb. "Airbnb's Nondiscrimination Policy: Our Commitment to Inclusion and Respect." *Airbnb*, n.d., airbnb.com. Accessed 19 Mar. 2019.

8. Flynn, "Can Airbnb Fix Its Discrimination Problem?"

9. Amy B. Wang. "Refusing to Sell Homes to Gay People Is Okay, GOP Congressman Says. Realtors Disagree." *Washington Post*, 26 May 2018, washingtonpost.com. Accessed 19 Mar. 2019.

10. Fred Barbash. "Federal Fair Housing Law Protects LGBT Couples, Court Rules for First Time." *Washington Post*, 6 Apr. 2017, washingtonpost.com. Accessed 19 Mar. 2019.

11. Barbash, "Federal Fair Housing Law Protects LGBT Couples."

12. Movement Advancement Project. "Non-Discrimination Laws." *Movement Advancement Project*, 18 Mar. 2019, lgbtmap.org. Accessed 19 Mar. 2019.

13. "H.R. 1447—115th Congress (2017–2018)." *US Congress*, 21 Mar. 2017, congress.gov. Accessed 19 Mar. 2019.

CHAPTER 7. THE CRIMINAL JUSTICE SYSTEM

1. "Unjust: How the Broken Criminal Justice System Fails LGBT People." *Center for American Progress* and *Movement Advancement Project*, 2016, lgbtmap.org. Accessed 19 Mar. 2019.

2. "Unjust: How the Broken Criminal Justice System Fails LGBT People."

3. Blake Thorkelson. "Transgender Mother Tells of Challenges to Parental Rights." *Yale News*, 2 Dec. 2016, news.yale.edu. Accessed 19 Mar. 2019.

4. Lambda Legal. "Rhines v. Young." *Lambda Legal*, n.d., lambdalegal.org. Accessed 19 Mar. 2019.

5. "Unjust: How the Broken Criminal Justice System Fails LGBT People."

6. Julie Moreau. "Bureau of Prisons Rolls Back Obama-Era Transgender Inmate Protections." *NBC News*, 14 May 2018, nbcnews.com. Accessed 19 Mar. 2019.

7. Jenny Gathright. "The Guidelines for Protection of Transgender Prisoners Just Got Rewritten." *NPR*, 12 May 2018, npr.org. Accessed 19 Mar. 2019.

8. Moreau, "Bureau of Prisons Rolls Back Obama-era Transgender Inmate Protections."

9. Moreau, "Bureau of Prisons Rolls Back Obama-era Transgender Inmate Protections."

CHAPTER 8. EFFECTS OF DISCRIMINATION

1. American Psychological Association. "Stress in America: The Impact of Discrimination." *Stress in America Survey*, 2016, apa.org. Accessed 19 Mar. 2019.

2. Human Rights Campaign. "Growing Up LGBT in America." *Human Rights Campaign*, 2012, hrc.org. Accessed 19 Mar. 2019.

3. Susan Kuklin. *Beyond Magenta: Transgender Teens Speak Out*. Candlewick, 2014. 113.

4. Kuklin, *Beyond Magenta*, 121–144.

5. Michael Friedman. "The Psychological Impact of LGBT Discrimination." *Psychology Today*, 11 Feb. 2014, psychologytoday.com. Accessed 19 Mar. 2019.

6. Movement Advancement Project. "New Report: Bisexual People Face Invisibility, Isolation, and Shocking Rates of Discrimination and Violence." *Movement Advancement Project*, 27 Sept. 2016, lgbtmap.org. Accessed 19 Mar. 2019.

7. Johnsen Del Rosario and The kNOw Youth Media. "Bisexual Erasure Is a Thing (Even within the LGBT Community)." *YR Media*, 8 Jan. 2018, yr.media. Accessed 19 Mar. 2019.

8. Ryan Thoreson. "'Like Walking through a Hailstorm': Discrimination against LGBT Youth in US Schools." *Human Rights Watch*, n.d., hrw.org. Accessed 19 Mar. 2019.

9. American Psychological Association. "Stress in America."

10. Charles Radcliffe. "The Real Cost of LGBT Discrimination." *World Economic Forum*, 5 Jan. 2016, weforum.org. Accessed 19 Mar. 2019.

11. Amy Elisa Jackson. "20 Companies that Champion LGBTQ Equality Hiring Now." *Glassdoor*, 6 June 2018, glassdoor.com. Accessed 19 Mar. 2019.

12. Camila Domonoske. "AP Calculates North Carolina's 'Bathroom Bill' Will Cost More Than $3.7 Billion." *NPR*, 27 Mar. 2017, npr.org. Accessed 19 Mar. 2019.

CHAPTER 9. FIGHTING AGAINST DISCRIMINATION

1. "HRC Story: Mission Statement." *Human Rights Campaign*, n.d., hrc.org. Accessed 19 Mar. 2019.

2. "Values." *Transgender Law Center*, n.d., transgenderlawcenter.org. Accessed 19 Mar. 2019.

3. Megan Townsend. "GLAAD's 'Where We Are on TV' Report Shows Television Telling More LGBTQ Stories Than Ever." *GLAAD*, 25 Oct. 2018, glaad.org. Accessed 19 Mar. 2019.

4. "Overview of Findings." *GLAAD*, 2018, glaad.org. Accessed 19 Mar. 2019.

5. "It Gets Better: Dan and Terry." *YouTube*, uploaded by It Gets Better Project, 21 Sept. 2010, youtube.com. Accessed 19 Mar. 2019.

6. "Welcome to the It Gets Better Project." *It Gets Better Project*, n.d., itgetsbetter.org. Accessed 19 Mar. 2019.

7. Paul Guzzo. "Transgender Community and Supporters Announce They Will Not Be Erased." *Tampa Bay Times*, 4 Nov. 2018, tampabay.com. Accessed 19 Mar. 2019.

8. Don Caldwell. "#WeWillNotBeErased." *Know Your Meme*, 2017, knowyourmeme.com. Accessed 19 Mar. 2019.

9. Les Fabian Brathwaite. "Less than 50% of Teens Identify as Straight, Says New Study." *Out Magazine*, 11 Mar. 2016, out.com. Accessed 19 Mar. 2019.

10. Eugene Scott. "In Farewell, Hatch Calls On Religious Conservatives to Find Common Ground with LGBT Community." *Washington Post*, 13 Dec. 2018, washingtonpost.com. Accessed 19 Mar. 2019.

11. Boris Dittrich. "The Future Is Not in Front of Us, It's Inside of Us." *Advocate*, 31 Aug. 2018, advocate.com. Accessed 19 Mar. 2019.

INDEX

Adams, Drew, 50
adoption, 17–18, 70
Affordable Care Act (ACA), 45
Airbnb, 60
American Academy of Pediatrics, 43
American Civil Liberties Union (ACLU), 39, 50, 84
American Medical Association, 43
American Psychological Association (APA), 12, 76, 83

BASE jumping, 34
Beyond I Do, 41, 56
Beyond Magenta: Transgender Teens Speak Out, 78
blood donation, 43
Bureau of Justice Statistics, 72
Bureau of Prisons, Federal, 74
Burts, Taylor TeMonet, 97

Center for American Progress, 42
Centers for Disease Control and Prevention, 97
Cheng, Philip J., 42–43
Civil Rights Act of 1964, 26
Colorado Civil Rights Commission, 18
Coming Out Matters, 95
Congress, US, 16, 22, 48, 62, 64, 72
Contreras, Krista and Jami, 41
cortisol, 82
Court of Appeals for the Eleventh Circuit, US, 31, 32, 33
Court of Appeals for the Second Circuit, US, 34
Court of Appeals for the Seventh Circuit, US, 33, 63, 64
Cox, Laverne, 68, 97
Crenshaw, Kimberlé, 12

Davids, Sharice, 22
Democratic Party, 19, 24
Department of Defense, US, 22–23
Department of Education, US, 16, 24–25, 46
Department of Health and Human Services (HHS), US, 20, 24, 45
Department of Housing and Urban Development, US, 58
Department of Justice, US, 16, 18, 35
direct discrimination, 9–11

District Court for the Southern District of Georgia, US, 31, 32
Dittrich, Boris, 99
Don't Ask, Don't Tell (DADT), 22, 90
"Don't Say Gay" laws, 54–55
Drubel, Jonny, 95
Dye, Jessi, 30, 31

Elliott, Byshop, 4–7
Ellis, Rowan, 78
Equal and Fair Housing Act of 2017, 64
Equal Employment Opportunity Commission (EEOC), 14, 26, 31
Evans, Jameka, 29–30, 31, 32, 33, 35
Evans v. Georgia Regional Hospital, 32

Fair Housing Act, 59, 62, 64, 65
First Amendment, 7, 20, 50
Fisher, Buddy, 60
Food and Drug Administration, US, 43
Free CeCe!, 68
Fricke, Aaron, 7
Funk, Liv, 46, 48

Gay and Lesbian Medical Association, 94
gay-straight alliance. *See* gender-sexuality alliance
gender-sexuality alliance (GSA), 6, 7, 94
GLAAD, 92
Glassdoor, 85
GLSEN, 48–49, 94
Gorsuch, Neil, 72

Hall, Hilde, 38–39
Harvard University, 12, 16, 36, 39, 41
Hatch, Orrin, 98
health care, 25, 36–45, 68, 72, 74, 85, 88, 90–91, 94
health insurance, 42–43, 44–45, 85
Hicklin, Jessica, 73–74
Hively, Kimberly, 33
homeless shelters, 58, 68, 79
hormone replacement therapy (HRT), 36, 38, 42, 73–74
House Bill 2 (HB2), 86–87
House of Representatives, US, 48, 65
Houston Press, 60
Huffpost, 52
human immunodeficiency virus (HIV), 40, 42, 43, 54, 55, 59, 90–91

Human Rights Campaign (HRC), 25, 30, 43, 76, 88, 90, 91, 97
Human Rights Watch, 75, 99

indirect discrimination, 11–12
It Gets Better Project, 95
Ivy Tech Community College, 33

Kahle, Sunnie, 52–53
Kaine, Tim, 64
Kavanaugh, Brett, 72
Kuklin, Susan, 78–79

Lambda Legal, 31, 50, 64, 90, 91
landlords, 10, 56, 59, 62, 64
Lawrence v. Texas, 70
Lhamon, Catherine E., 25
Log Cabin Republicans (LCR), 24
Lynn, Jessica, 70–71

Manning, Chelsea, 97
Masterpiece Cakeshop, 18, 20,
Masterpiece Cakeshop v. Colorado Civil Rights Commission, 18
McDonald, CeCe, 68
McKinley High School, 4, 7
McLemore, Megan, 75
mental health, 13, 30, 68, 76, 82, 83
Miracle Hill, 20
Missouri Department of Corrections (MDOC), 73–74
Moore, Raymond P., 63
Moore, William Allen, 34

National Inmate Survey, 66
National School Climate Survey, 48–49, 51
NBC News, 34
New York Civil Liberties Union, 4
New York Times, 43, 45, 97
North Bend High School (NBHS), 46–48

Oakley, Tyler, 78
Obama, Barack, 22–23, 25, 28, 45, 74
Obamacare. *See* Affordable Care Act
Obergefell v. Hodges, 22
Oregon Department of Education (ODE), 46
Out & Equal, 94–95

PayPal, 85, 87
Pentagon. *See* Department of Defense, US
PFLAG, 84
Phillips, Jack, 18

physical health, 12–13, 38, 40–41, 54–55, 79, 82
Potosi Correctional Center (PCC), 73
pre-exposure prophylaxis (PrEP), 40, 43
Pride, 60
private schools, 52, 53
prom, 4–7, 9
public schools, 6–7, 20, 24, 50, 52, 53, 54

religious exemptions, 20, 91
Religious Freedom Restoration Act, 74
Remedy: Queer and Trans Voices on Health and Health Care, The, 38
Republican Party, 19, 24
Rhines, Charles, 71

Savage, Dan, 95
Senate, US, 48, 65, 98
Smith, Hailey, 46
Smith, Rachel and Tonya, 62–63
sodomy, 70
solitary confinement, 72
Stacy, David, 43
stress, 13, 76, 79, 82, 83
Student Nondiscrimination Act, 48
Supreme Court, US, 18, 22–23, 26, 31, 32, 35, 70, 71, 72, 90

Thompson, Doris, 52–53
Timberlake Christian School (TCS), 52–53
Title IX, 53–54
Title VII, 26, 31, 33, 34–35, 54, 62
Trans Day of Visibility, 97
Transgender Law Center, 91
Transgender Offender Manual, 74, 75
Trevor Project, 84
Trump, Donald, 16, 20, 22–23, 24, 25, 28, 44–45, 72, 97, 99

Urban Institute, 59
US Transgender Survey, 38
US Youth Risk Behavior Survey, 82

wage gap, 28
Washington Post, 63
Wetzel, Martha, 63, 64
Williams Institute, 79
World Economic Forum, 84

YouTube, 78, 95

Zarda, Donald, 33, 34

ABOUT THE AUTHORS

DUCHESS HARRIS, JD, PHD

Dr. Harris is a professor of American Studies at Macalester College and curator of the Duchess Harris Collection of ABDO books. She is also the coauthor of the titles in the collection, which features popular selections such as *Hidden Human Computers: The Black Women of NASA* and series including News Literacy and Being Female in America.

Before working with ABDO, Dr. Harris authored several other books on the topics of race, culture, and American history. She served as an associate editor for *Litigation News*, the American Bar Association Section of Litigation's quarterly flagship publication, and was the first editor in chief of *Law Raza*, an interactive online journal covering race and the law, published at William Mitchell College of Law. She has earned a PhD in American Studies from the University of Minnesota and a JD from William Mitchell College of Law.

KRISTIN MARCINIAK

Kristin Marciniak lives in Overland Park, Kansas, with her husband, son, and very vocal golden retriever. When she's not writing about being LGBTQ in America, she can be found piecing quilts, knitting socks, baking bread, and trying to master crossovers on her roller skates.